Praise for Crisis Contemplation

"*Crisis Contemplation* should be on the reading list of theological educators as we reclaim physical spaces that we abandoned and interpersonal relationships that we have sought to maintain during the COVID-19 crisis. Dr. Holmes reminds us that the present moment cannot be extracted from historical and current crises that have been 'precipitated by oppression, violence, pandemics, abuses of power, or natural disasters and planetary disturbances.' She takes us on a 'luminous' womanist theo-poetic journey away from 'COVID-19 anti-scientific politics' so that we open ourselves to futurism and cosmic rebirthing. We are invited to remember 'our cosmic origins' and embrace mysticism as part of everyday life. The book can be used in ecclesial and academic classrooms or by individuals—anyone ready to engage in crisis contemplation to discern the 'moves of an active Holy Spirit.' In her words, 'When crisis is the context for the past and present, hopeful people manage the now and imagine a future.'"

—Marcia Y. Riggs, PhD,
J. Erskine Professor of Christian Ethics,
Columbia Theological Seminary

"If you or your community have been feeling the anxieties of the current global crises then this book is for you. Barbara Holmes spotlights the intersection of communal crisis and contemplation and illuminates how this journey may be the only path toward real transformation."

—Dr. Donald Bryant, Jr.,
Founder and Lead Pastor of ONE Community Church

"'Whether we like it or not, our personal destiny is interwoven with the wellbeing of the community. After each crisis, questions loom. Will we rise to the occasion and allow the planet to recover from our toxic greed or will we continue to destroy our planet, our only home?' Barbara Holmes asks this question for all the bridge crossers and those on the threshold, and she speaks my own heart and mind so eloquently in this prophetic vision of our unfolding."

—Therese Taylor-Stinson,
Author-Editor, Community Organizer, and Founding Managing
Member of the Spiritual Directors of Color Network

"I and others always knew there had to be more paths to something as good and necessary as contemplation. We concluded that there were two universal and foundational paths of transformation: *great suffering* and *great love*. Finally, Barbara Holmes makes it clear to us that we might just be right! She wisely names the universally available path: 'crisis contemplation.' Barbara has democratized this inner journey with convincing prose and effective practices. Love and suffering are the ultimate crises for the human ego."

—Richard Rohr, OFM,
Author, Founder of the Center for Action and Contemplation
(CAC), and Dean of CAC's Living School

Crisis Contemplation

CRISIS CONTEMPLATION

Healing the Wounded Village

Barbara A. Holmes

CAC PUBLISHING
Center for Action and Contemplation
cac.org

Requests for information should be addressed to:
CAC Publishing
PO Box 12464
Albuquerque, NM 87195

Cover design: Nelson Kane and Nicholas Kramer
Interior design: Nelson Kane
Cover illustration by David Klein

PUBLISHER'S CATALOGING-IN-PUBLICATION DATA
(Prepared by The Donohue Group, Inc.)

Names: Holmes, Barbara Ann, 1943- author.
Title: Crisis contemplation : healing the wounded village / Barbara A. Holmes.
Description: Albuquerque, NM : CAC PUBLISHING, Center for Action and
      Contemplation, [2021] | Includes bibliographical references.
Identifiers: ISBN 9781623050559 (paperback)
Subjects: LCSH: Spiritual healing. | Contemplation. | Crises--Social
      aspects. | Crises--Psychological aspects. | Communities--Religious
      aspects. | Psychic trauma.
Classification: LCC BL65.M4 H65 2021 | DDC 203.1--dc23

Printed in the United States of America

This book is dedicated:

To the fallen and wounded

Rest

To the future soon-coming

Hurry!

To the children who imagine more

Don't get weary

To the hope and healing on its way

Don't delay

And to my husband, George: my village, my love, my inspiration

The possible has been tried and failed.

Now it's time to try the impossible.

—Sun Ra

CONTENTS

PREFACE

What Is Crisis Contemplation?

At the center of every crisis
is an inner space
so deep, so beckoning,
so suddenly and daringly vast,
that it feels like a universe,
feels like God.

When the unthinkable happens,
and does not relent,
we fall through our hubris
toward an inner flow,
an abiding and rebirthing darkness
that feels like home.[1]

---

1. Italicized poetry and prose poetry without a cited author or footnote are my own.

T HE LAST THING that we want to talk about during a crisis is the crisis itself. Folks are nervous enough. I am writing this book about crisis in communal contexts after the emergence of COVID-19, police murders of unarmed black and brown people in the streets, and environmental disasters.

While the year 2020 was devastating, it was not unique. Throughout human history, there have been cycles of wellbeing and catastrophe. This book is not about one crisis-filled year, but about the many entry points into contemplation, including the portal of communal crisis. As you might guess, when the crisis is upon us and the "ordinary" collapses, life gets complicated very quickly.

I first recognized crisis contemplation as I was writing the first edition of *Joy Unspeakable: Contemplative Practices of the Black Church* in 2004. As I considered the intense state of suffering experienced by Africans of many tribes and nations in the holds of slave ships during the trauma of the Middle Passage, I recognized the formation of a village of sorts. Strangers were linked by destiny, chains, and moans that focused their intentions on survival, resiliency, and inner strength. Together, their moans created a spiritual bulwark, a contemplative space of respite in the midst of unrelenting pain, death, and separation.

Not much has changed in terms of our communal response to crises. Once the unthinkable crisis has us in its clutches, we have no choice but to let go of our false sense of control and ride the waves of destiny. On the other side of this wild ride awaits extinction, resurrection, or rebirth. There are no other options. The following chapters offer a roadmap for discovery, spiritual mapping, remembrance, and options for healing trauma.

Chapter 1—Crisis describes the shattering event: the pandemic or earthquake, the systematic abuse of one group or another, that triggers the crisis. **Chapter 2—Contemplation** explores communal contemplative experiences that arise as a result of rupture and the shift from a familiar reality to the unknown. **Chapter 3—Wounds** focuses on trauma in historical, intergenerational, and epigenetic contexts during and after the crisis. **Chapter 4—The Village Response** concerns itself with communal formation, belonging, resistance, and resilience.

Chapter 5—Healing focuses on recovery of memory and story, revival of culture and ritual, and the performance of joy. Finally, **Chapter**

6—Futurism and Cosmic Rebirth explores crisis contemplation as a gift of liminality and an opportunity for bio-spiritual resurrection.

This book is not meant to be read cover to cover without pause. Contemplative moments will arise as you read it, as they did for me as I wrote it. Take a moment to consider what crisis contemplation means for the groups described in these chapters and for your own life as an individual who is associated with various villages of origin and choice. There are questions at the end of each chapter for reflection and discussion.

Preface Practices

1. In terms of genetics and geography, who are your people? Describe yourself and your people in one paragraph, without references to "white," "black," "brown," or any other color-related social designation.
2. How did you come to know your genetic linkages and origins? Was it through family history, DNA tests, or some other source? What in the findings has surprised, disappointed, and/or empowered you? Did anything in your DNA report change your sense of self?
3. Write an "identity prayer" for you and your people. Honor their sacrifices with your silence or your songs and breathe your blessing upon their journey and yours.

ACKNOWLEDGMENTS

I'm trying to speak—to write—the truth. I'm trying to be clear. I'm not interested in being fancy, or even original. Clarity and truth will be plenty, if I can only achieve them.

—Octavia E. Butler, *Parable of the Sower*

IN THIS BOOK, I am describing the contours of crisis contemplation, a spiritual event that arises from calamity rather than comfort. More than a practice, it is a state of being that is experienced by a group of people who may or may not share origins, values, and communal or village ties. I am describing something elusive, but real and worthy of our attention.

I am grateful for mentors and friends who continue to encourage this work, including but not limited to: The Revs. Gloria Roach Thomas, Sonia L. Walker, and Lisa Anderson; Drs. Marcia Y. Riggs, Jeanne Stevenson-Moessner, Lynne Westfield, Victor Anderson, Cheryl Kirk Duggan, Peter Gathje, Valerie Bridgeman, Lewis Baldwin, Anthea Butler, Frank Thomas, Emily Townes, Walter F. Brueggemann, and Katie Cannon. They taught me how to interpret, using the lens of this present age and the spiritual foundations of ages past. Also, more importantly, they encouraged me to find my own voice. Ultimately, my mentors and friends created a village around me and other upcoming scholars and mystics that was full of laughter, creativity, and intellectual integrity.

I am also grateful for the opportunities I've had to contribute to theological education and seminary leadership. Every student that I taught, taught me even more. In the spirit of "greater things shall you do" (see John 14:12), these former students excel as spiritual leaders and teachers: Rev. Drs. Andre Johnson, Earle Fisher, Christopher Davis, and Joyce Thomas.

I have recently joined the faculty of the Center for Action and Contemplation (CAC) under the leadership of Fr. Richard Rohr. What a joy to be able to combine African American mysticism with the transformational work of this community. When I look back on a lifetime of teaching and learning, I am thankful that I earned my degrees later in life. By then, I understood my gifts and my shortcomings, my call and my communities of accountability. Although I recognize the dynamic nature of the word "understanding," my point is that I pursued graduate studies when it was far too late to indoctrinate me into systems thinking.

I am brave when I write because I never write alone. My heart is too full of the remembrance of family and friends. My head is in constant communication with wise elders, still here and long gone. My spirit is too busy dancing through the wonder and the mysteries of life. Through it all, "I'm trying to speak—to write—the truth. I'm trying to be clear."

The moan is the birthing sound,
the first movement toward
a creative response to oppression,
the entry into the heart of
contemplation through the
crucible of crisis.

—Barbara Holmes, *Joy Unspeakable*

CHAPTER ONE

CRISIS

In every crisis there is a message. Crises are nature's way of forcing change—breaking down old structures, shaking loose negative habits so that something new and better can take their place.

—Susan L. Taylor

In the Beginning

THE CRISIS BEGINS without warning, shatters our assumptions about the way the world works, and changes our story and the stories of our neighbors. The reality that was so familiar to us is gone suddenly, and we don't know what is happening.

Where there is no understanding, we create it. When we are anxious about our lack of control, we conjure theories that quell our anxiety. The truth of the matter is that we live on a mysterious planet, with other living beings whose interiority and spiritual realities are just beyond our cognitive reach.

If life, as we experience it, is a fragile crystal orb that holds our daily routines and dreams of order and stability, then sudden and catastrophic crises shatter this illusion of normalcy. The crises discussed in this chapter are usually precipitated by circumstances beyond the ordinary. I am referring to oppression, violence, pandemics, abuses of power, or natural disasters and planetary disturbances.

Until the moment that the crisis begins, you feel relatively safe and situated. Suddenly, everything changes. You are stolen from your village, placed in chains, and loaded onto ships headed to the Americas to be sold as slaves. Or, you are rounded up, placed on trains headed for a German death camp: Auschwitz, Treblinka, Bergen-Belsen, or Dachau. Or, upon the orders of the US government, you and members of your tribe are rounded up to begin a forced march from native lands in North Carolina to Oklahoma. Or, without warning, they send you and other Asian neighbors to internment camps. In each circumstance, some of you will survive the experience, but many of you will not.

In Haiti, the ground opens as an earthquake swallows people, homes, and resources. Or, a hurricane of incredible magnitude slams into Puerto Rico's fragile infrastructure or New Orleans' vulnerable lands below sea level, and help does not come. Up until the moment of the disaster, you may be vaguely aware that your humanity has been politicized and disregarded, but there is no immediacy to this life-and-death issue until the crisis is upon you and your community.

A global pandemic is raging, yet toxic masculinity and anti-scientific politics in the US reject the wearing of protective masks and promote a return to work long before it is safe. In an election year, and to salvage the economy, citizens are called upon to "take one" for team USA.

The extent and magnitude of such crises can differ, but there are common elements. As a crisis reaches the point where we experience spiritual and psychic dissolution, contemplation takes the form of a freefall through our carefully woven safety nets of "normalcy." We let go of our narratives, our plans, the stories that we tell ourselves about who we are and where we come from. We toss our resumes or CVs to the winds and finally realize that, with regard to our corporate or social climbing, there is no "there" there. When a crisis impacts a community, we collectively plunge into a space of stillness and unknowing, a shared interiority of potential and spiritual rebirthing.

Signs of Trouble

WE CAN IDENTIFY three common elements in every crisis: The event is usually unexpected, the person or community is unprepared, and there is nothing that anyone could do to stop it from happening. Even if there are signs everywhere that something is not right, we tend to ignore the warnings and the signposts. Not even sky writing, or messengers from other worlds, would be able to shift our gaze from the comfort of our daily routines. Thus, the slave catchers, the roundups for native removal, the pandemics, devastating hurricanes, and volcanic eruptions catch us off guard. As for devastation that results from weather and natural disasters, we can track, predict, and warn, but we cannot control planetary forces.

When the unexpected happens during a communal crisis, we are not alone. We are with friends and neighboring villagers, and we all experience the same break in reality. Bereft of words, all of us hold the same question: How could this be happening?

Crisis of the One and the Many

I am an individual with a voice. I am also embedded in a community on which I'm highly dependent, from which I came, and to which I will return. And I include the community of the natural world in that. And I need both the chutzpah and the humility to be there fully, to be there now, and to be there in a life-giving way.

—Parker Palmer

WHEN I WRITE about a crisis of the one and the many, I am not addressing personal pain and suffering. This is not the story of the husband who takes you to dinner to ask for a divorce—unexpected, yes; catastrophic, maybe; but that is not what this book is about. This book is about the infliction of trauma upon a group or community that I will call "the village." Robert Franklin writes that "Neighborhoods become villages when all of the adults step up to show care and concern for all of the children."[1]

---

1. Robert M. Franklin, *Crisis in the Village: Restoring Hope in African American Communities* (Minneapolis: Fortress, 2007), 3.

I know what he is talking about. The street on which I lived as a child felt like a refuge. The multiple-family house that my dad and his brother bought after World War II was filled with family only: six apartments of aunties and uncles, cousins and other mothers. Neighbors watched and shared, gossiped and protected. Long before I understood the dangers beyond my neighborhood, I felt the love of people who differed in opinion, occupation, and goals, but who recognized the need for communal solidarity.

Most were familiar with crises as a result of a childhood in the American South, their migration North, or their experiences with discrimination and poverty. In a village or community, trauma may result from oppression based on group identity, religion, or immutable traits like ability, ethnicity, and/or gender/sexuality. Also, crisis can come from the chaos, destruction, and loss that nature or pandemics can unleash.

I am describing instances of mass trauma experienced by entire communities.

> The term . . . "mass trauma" . . . is conceptualized . . . as an event involving multiple people simultaneously experiencing, witnessing, or being confronted with actual and/or threatened death, serious injury, and threat to self or others. The most common examples of mass trauma typically involve natural disasters, . . . war and organized violence, [and] civil/political/community violence.[2]

So, what is the difference between a crisis of spirit and soul that affects individuals and the crises of communities that result from oppression or trauma? Since every community is comprised of individuals, the crises for individual members and the group carry horizons of the whole. They merge and intersect.

When the Crisis Is Personal

WHEN THE CRISIS is personal, individuals may suffer a dark night of the soul. The issues may be personal or faith-based. An individual's

2. Elizabeth Wieling and Mona Mittal, "JMFT Special Section on Mass Trauma," *Journal of Marital and Family Therapy* 34, no. 2 (April 15, 2008): 127, https://doi.org/10.1111/j.1752-0606.2008.00059.x.

crisis may include a sense of God-forsakenness, loss of identity, the struggle between God's will and ours, or may simply arise out of a basic tenet of the life journey: "In this life, you will have trouble" (John 16:33). As strange as it may seem, a crisis of the individual may be a means of stretching us toward our highest good! Even though it hurts, perhaps the crisis is a blessed opportunity to negotiate the wisdom patterns that Fr. Richard Rohr has identified as cycles of order, disorder, and reorder.[3]

I can't say with certainty, because I also am still on the journey, but I know from my own life experience that each personal crisis nudges us toward greater faith, greater resilience, and even greater compassion. This is not the way that humans prefer to learn, but to live with and through each crisis may be a divine gift with long-reaching effects.

When the Crisis Is Communal

OFTEN, A CRISIS of the community is inflicted by an event, entity, or system. It can be a devastating and destructive divergence from our ordinary lives. Nothing can be learned from a genocide or holocaust other than the human potential for unspeakable cruelty and our ability to survive together.

When a crisis shatters the community and our pleas for divine help go unanswered, individual heroism will not save the day. Leaders usually arise during times of trouble, but they cannot stop the crisis from happening. Instead, they act as representatives of the stricken group, inspire resistance and resilience, and organize responses.

For me, Nelson Mandela, Sitting Bull, Harriet Tubman, Óscar Romero, Sojourner Truth, and others come to mind. Perhaps you are Harriet Tubman (d. 1913), hiding and trying to make it to Canada with members of your community. Perhaps you are a person of color today wondering when the "powers that be" will decide to put your village in peril.

---

3. Richard Rohr, *The Wisdom Pattern: Order, Disorder, Reorder* (Cincinnati: Franciscan Media, 2020).

It is the village that enters into crisis. No matter how tenuous and invisible the bonds of a particular village may be, members of the group must, for their safety, survival, and transformation, cling to, rely upon, and respond out of shared communal wisdom and contemplative reorientation. The crisis changes the life space and our reality structures. It removes all ordinary options for relief.

Only questions bubble to the surface:

1. Where is the God who heard our prayers in ages past?
2. Where are the authority figures, the people upon whom we relied to create order and safety?
3. Will I ever see my family, my country, my home again?

The Loss of Control and Agency

WE DON'T CONTROL very much, but we think that we do! If we are honest, we would admit that even self-control is fleeting and occasional, yet we truly believe that control of others and our environment is possible. It is intoxicating to believe that we can bend the moral arc of the universe to suit our preferences, when we demonstrably cannot.[4] Yes, we can influence outcomes by resisting oppression and by leaping toward a transformed future, but our efforts do not guarantee the results that we want. A crisis of the one and the many shocks us into another reality, where the ordinary isn't ordinary anymore.

When a community is in crisis, there are specific events that may occur. Initially, there is rupture, the displacement of all that is familiar. The endings and beginnings are abrupt. Even though there may have been subtle signs and warnings that have gone unheeded, the moment of shattering is usually unexpected.

Those targeted are usually unprepared to respond and there is nothing that can be done to stop the event from happening, other than the unlikely change of heart of those inflicting the trauma, or the redirection

---

4. Ellen J. Langer, "The Illusion of Control," *Journal of Personality and Social Psychology* 32, no. 2 (1975): 311–328, https://doi.org/10.1037/0022-3514.32.2.311.

of a hurricane, or a vaccine that stops a pandemic in its tracks. There is no one-size-fits-all crisis. There are no easy solutions.

Crises can occur as a result of well-meaning attempts to assure social order. As Michelle Alexander has noted, mass incarceration is a tragedy, a crisis, and the precursor to a new type of slavery.[5] The relentless killing of black and brown bodies by the police impacts individuals, but is also a communal crisis with health and social implications for everyone. Each communal crisis has individual, but also collective, characteristics and consequences.

When the crisis comes, communities experience emotional, physical, and psychological trauma together, without the opportunity for immediate resolution or relief. Always, there is the shattering of equilibrium, the shift from balanced exchanges of discontent to the ultimate decimation of the social order and the environment.

Planetary/Environmental and Health Crises

Today, our common planetary home is falling into ruin. We are on the brink of an unprecedented global challenge regarding the sustainability of our common home, which places a question mark on the very future of human civilization.[6]

WHEN THE CRISIS is environmental, planetary, or health related, we tend to blame disasters on the capriciousness of nature. Inevitably, we learn that a lack of respectful interaction with our planet, human pollution, and exploitation can trigger seemingly "natural" disasters. The myth of human dominion and the elevation of the self over the planet and its co-inhabitants is a loss for all of us—but more than a loss, it is a crisis.

For African diasporan people in America, connections to nature and the land are often conflicted. People escaping to the North considered

---

5. Michelle Alexander, *The New Jim Crow: Mass Incarceration in the Age of Colorblindness* (New York: New Press, 2012).

6. Joshtrom Isaac Kureethadam, "Our Common Planetary Home," *Center for Action and Contemplation*, May 17, 2020, https://cac.org/our-common-planetary-home-2020-05-17/.

nature an obstacle that stood between them and their freedom. It was also a place where lynching and other acts of random violence were inflicted upon their communities. As black folks toiled in cotton fields that they did not own and ran through swamps to escape slave-hunting dogs, they lost their ability to relate to the natural world as an intrinsic element of an inspirited community.

Slowly, current generations are retrieving their connections to nature. After all, it was not the land that enslaved Africans in the Diaspora, it was the colonizers and supremacists who fueled this estrangement. Historically, indigenous people related to the land as an integral part of the community. Nature provided healing herbs, food, and other resources. By contrast, colonizers tended to consider both land and people commodities to be bought and sold. It is time to reorder our priorities if life is to continue to thrive on this planet.

Right now, the planet is responding to its abuse and neglect, our consumerism and rapaciousness with melting ice caps, global warming, raging forest fires, the spread of animal infections to human populations, and widespread species extinctions.

> I'd like to see a collective awakening to the . . . realities we face as a species, as an ecosystem of countless life forms. So far, humans have found only one viable home out in the infinite cosmos. If we're not careful, if we don't wake up to the warnings, we humans are about to be homeless.[7]

It is a particular type of madness to destroy the only known planet that supports human life! Moreover, when we prioritize our destructive lifestyles over the health of the planet, we are rejecting the s(S)pirit of God that is alive and interwoven throughout creation.

---

7. Li Sumpter, "Using Afrofuturism to Build the Kind of World You Want," *EcoWurd*, November 19, 2018, https://ecowurd.com/2018/11/19/using-afrofuturism-to-build-the-kind-of-world-you-want/.

Mupasi: The Cosmic s(S)pirit[8]

> *Mupasi* is understood as cosmic spirit, the axis of the universe apprehended as an organic whole. The web of life was brought into being, is sustained by, and inhabited by *Mupasi* . . . . [This enlivening s(S)pirit] presents an ecological critique that is meaningful for a renewed appreciation of community beyond an anthropocentric focus. The cosmic relatedness brings a renewed vision of the universe as a cosmic community of the s(S)pirit.[9]

THEOLOGIAN KUZIPA NALWAMBA introduces us to the concept of *Mupasi*: the Cosmic s(S)pirit. She writes that this vital spiritual force seamlessly weaves the lives of earth's inhabitants into an "inseparable bond that makes reality one whole, and lends kinship to all creatures."[10] She reminds us that this cosmic s(S)pirit is an inbreaking force of vitality and empowerment that is not unique to one culture or belief system.

We find this vitality in "the Chinese notion of *chi*, the Egyptian concept of *maat*, the Japanese notion of *ki* and the Hindu idea of *prana*."[11] Through Nalwamba's lens, life in community includes animals, land, flora, and the elements. The cosmic spirit does not allow for any separation between "environment, society and the spiritual."[12] Rather, we are reminded that human beings are a part of a community of inspired life. Moreover, the earth, rather than being an inert commodity available for our exploitation, is part of a universe understood to be an organic whole. Oh, how we need a visitation of the s(S)spirit as a cyclical and necessary infusion of a God-given, life-sustaining force!

---

8. Dr. Kuzipa M. B. Nalwamba tells me that "the s(S) indicates continuities and discontinuities (without conflating) in references to spirit and Holy Spirit in the Bible and, by extension, spirit in other knowledge systems, including other religions." She wrote to me, "I found it helpful for undergirding the argument about the interrelatedness with the cosmic community of life in God's *oikos*." Text messages dated August 11–13, 2020.

9. Kuzipa M. B. Nalwamba, "*Mupasi* as Cosmic s(S)pirit: The Universe as a Community of Life," *HTS Teologiese Studies/Theological Studies* 73, no. 3 (August 23, 2017): abstract, https://doi.org/10.4102/hts.v73i3.4624.

10. Nalwamba, 1.

11. Nalwamba, 2.

12. P. J. Nel, "Morality and Religion in African Thought," *Acta Theologica* 28, no. 2 (2008): 37, https://www.ajol.info//index.php/actat/article/view/48880.

Many Western societies have either lost touch with the s(S)pirit or have tried to domesticate its influence in our lives. Fortunately, the holiness of the s(S)pirit continues to gush forth from a wild and creative source. We need only turn to the Bible for verification that when the s(S)pirit appears there are dramatic changes to the status quo.

When the s(S)pirit descends upon the upper room, there are reports of flaming tongues and seemingly drunk disciples (Acts 2:1-13). Right after Jesus' baptism, the s(S)pirit sends him into the desert to be tempted. When that wild bird enters the scene, surprises abound. To reconnect to this primal source of renewal, we may have to recover our cultural origins.

If, as scientists suggest, we are all Africa's children,[13] it seems reasonable to introduce this Afrocentric cosmological approach that speaks to the unitive reality of life on planet Earth and in the universe. Nalwamba closes her article with the assertion that "God . . . gives life *(ruach)* as a layered, coexistent way of be-ing that transcends material-spiritual binaries. It also casts humans as ontologically related to the rest of creation."[14]

The real question is whether or not we are willing to host the mystery of other beings who have their own unique embodiment. Cosmologist Brian Swimme reminds us that,

> A tree is a self: it is "unseen shaping" more than it is leaves or bark, roots or cellulose or fruit. . . . What this means is that we must address trees as we must address all things, confronting them in the awareness that we are in the presence of numinous mystery.[15]

To engage that "unseen shaping" in the environment, we must also recognize its movement within us and our communities. We are not creatures of our own making. We are shaped by our genetic coding, our

---

13. Scientists and researchers tell us that "humans first evolved in Africa, and much of human evolution occurred on that continent. The fossils of early humans who lived between 6 and 2 million years ago come entirely from Africa. Early humans first migrated out of Africa into Asia probably between 2 million and 1.8 million years ago." "Human Evolution," *Smithsonian National Museum of Natural History*, https://naturalhistory.si.edu/education/teaching-resources/social-studies/human-evolution#.

14. Nalwamba, 7.

15. Brian Swimme, *The Universe Is a Green Dragon: A Cosmic Creation Story* (Philadelphia: Bear & Company, 1984), 130.

environment (families and communities), and the breath of God. For good measure, we are accompanied by an indwelling Holy Spirit who leads and guides us into all truth (John 16:13). Nalwamba describes a mystery that deserves our wonder and respect if we are to thrive in an environment that requires cooperative coexistence.

In the next section, we encounter catastrophic environmental and health crises.

Wade in the Water—New Orleans and Puerto Rico

> When you pass through the waters, I will be with you;
> and through the rivers, they shall not overwhelm you;
> when you walk through fire you shall not be burned,
> and the flame shall not consume you.
>
> —Isaiah 43:2

ISAIAH IS NOT speaking for himself. He is voicing a promise of the Creator, a promise that can be relied upon throughout the ages. If this is true, how do we understand the flooding of New Orleans after Hurricane Katrina, and the devastation of Puerto Rico after Hurricane Maria? I don't have any easy answers, but I want to suggest a contemplative interpretation of Isaiah 43:2 through the lens of the commandment to "love your neighbor as yourself" (Mark 12:31).

I am convinced that devastating hurricanes do not represent a failure of the prophet's promise on behalf of a living God, but a neighbor-to-neighbor failure. It was the failure of governments and political parties to understand the circumstances of poor and underserved people of color/culture living on the margins in vulnerable geographic locations that exacerbated the effects of the hurricanes.

According to reports, most of the deaths in New Orleans and Puerto Rico occurred after the hurricanes struck. As ubiquitous as cars are in American society, most of the poor in New Orleans relied on public transportation and did not own cars. In Puerto Rico, a historically weakened infrastructure, difficult terrain, and oppressive US politics made the crisis worse.

We are told to love our neighbors, but how can we love them when we don't know them or their circumstances? Eventually, the abandoned populace sheltered in the New Orleans Convention Center without food or water, waiting for Godot,[16] while Puerto Ricans in rural areas hunkered down in survival mode. Poet, journalist, and professor at Columbia University Ed Morales wrote,

> The . . . delay in sending real aid to Puerto Rico after Hurricane Maria is a distasteful display of colonialist racism. But it's par for the course: our [Puerto Rican] citizenship has always been second-class.[17]

Morales is referring to the legacy of US colonialism that reached from the past into the present day after Maria hit the island. Most Americans are unaware of the historically separate and unequal treatment of the island.

> Going back as far as the 1901 case *Downes v. Bidwell*, decided by some of the judges who ruled on *Plessy v. Ferguson*, a new colonial turn of phrase entered the American vocabulary. Puerto Rico should not be considered fit for becoming a state in the Union, but would be instead an "unincorporated territory" "belonging to, but not part of," the United States.[18]

The crises in Puerto Rico and in New Orleans had as much to do with racism, ethnocentrism, and neglect as with the forces of nature. What we know is that the United States of America has the capacity (if not the will) to address the needs of all its people. However, in each of these geocultural locations, our government failed to rise to the occasion.[19]

---

16. *Waiting for Godot* is the title of a play written by Samuel Beckett. The play is a typical example of the Theatre of the Absurd, and people use the phrase "waiting for Godot" to describe a situation where people are waiting for something that will probably never come.

17. Ed Morales, "Puerto Rico: Belonging to, But Not Part of," *NACLA*, September 29, 2017, https://nacla.org/news/2017/09/29/puerto-rico-belonging-not-part.

18. Morales.

19. Per Helio Fred Garcia:

"New Orleans flooded on a Monday. Throughout that day and Tuesday, the government kept assuring the news media that FEMA and other agencies were on the

A collective crisis needs a collective response. Layers of past collective trauma are being reactivated during this time of strong uncertainty. In this time of heightened emotions, we can diligently apply practices which will deepen our sense of presence and grounding within ourselves and within the greater collective we share.[20]

Whether we like it or not, our personal destiny is interwoven with the wellbeing of the community. After each crisis, questions loom. Will we rise to the occasion and allow the planet to recover from our toxic greed or will we continue to destroy our planet, our only home?

---

ground and helping the victims. But news coverage showed little federal presence except for U.S. Coast Guard helicopter rescues. [There were] no staging areas for victims; no shelters; but hundreds of people, mostly African-American, struggling against the rising waters and without help. On Tuesday the news media persistently questioned why there was little evidence of federal help for the city, noting even that dead bodies continued to float by.

"On that Wednesday the media not only covered the lack of a FEMA presence on the ground, but also how FEMA prevented or stalled potential aid from other sources. For example, a fourteen-car caravan arranged by the sheriff of Loudoun County, Virginia, carrying supplies of water and food, was not allowed into the city. FEMA stopped tractor trailers carrying water to the supply staging area in Alexandria, Louisiana because they did not have the necessary paperwork. CNN also reported that during the weekend before the flood Mayor Nagin had made a call for firefighters to help with rescue operations. But as firefighters from across the country arrived to help victims, they were first sent by FEMA to Atlanta for a day long training program in community relations and sexual harassment. When they arrived in New Orleans, the volunteer firefighters were permitted only to give out flyers with FEMA number, but were forbidden from engaging in rescue operations. The media reported not only the resentment felt by the first responders, but also how FEMA's policies hurt those people who were begging for aid in New Orleans.

"That day Homeland Security Secretary Michael Chertoff held a press conference in which he said, 'We are extremely pleased with every element of the federal government, all of our federal partners, have made to this terrible tragedy.' That day Mayor Ray Nagin went on the radio and blasted the federal government for its failure to respond quickly."

Helio Fred Garcia, "Crisis Management Lessons Ten Years After Hurricane Katrina," *Logos Consulting Group*, August 29, 2015, https://logosconsulting.net/crisis-management-lessons-ten-years-after-hurricane-katrina/.

20. Thomas Hübl, "Deepening Our Collective Roots," *Tricycle*, March 13, 2020, https://tricycle.org/trikedaily/coronavirus-meditations/?#thomashubl.

The Crisis of Worldwide Pandemics

Epidemics are a category of disease that seem to hold up the mirror
to human beings as to who we really are.[21]

IN THE YEAR 2020, the COVID-19 pandemic swept the globe, taking lives
and overwhelming healthcare systems, world markets, political agendas,
and expectations of normalcy. It was not the first pandemic to threaten
everyone in the world, but it was the first to galvanize anti-scientific politics. In the United States, it exposed the selfishness of radical individual-
ism, as mask-wearing to prevent the spread of the virus was politicized.

With a US election looming in the fall of 2020, a scattered and anemic
national response to COVID-19 left states with rising infection rates, few
options, and even fewer resources as restaurants closed, many school cam-
puses went to remote learning, and families were required to quarantine.

As Fr. Richard Rohr notes in one of his pandemic meditations:

Humanity, you are all One.
You are one beloved community,
and you are one global sickness.
You are all contagious—and always have been,
unconsciously infecting and yet able to also bless one another.[22]

Fr. Rohr reminds us that blaming one virus or another for our circumstances makes no sense when we are all contagious, infecting not just
one another, but also our environment, the Earth, and our current reality.
The good news is that we also embody the potential to forgive, love, and
bless our neighbors.

During the height of the pandemic, some insisted that the virus would
just "disappear after a while." Kerry Maloney, Harvard Divinity School's

21. Frank M. Snowden, as quoted by Christine Jeske, "This Pandemic Hits Americans Where We're Spiritually Weak," *Christianity Today*, May 7, 2020, https://www.
christianitytoday.com/ct/2020/may-web-only/coronavirus-pandemic-hits-ameri-
cans-spiritually-weak.html.

22. Richard Rohr, "It Seems We Now Require Some Necessary Falling," *Center for
Action and Contemplation*, October 20, 2020.

chaplain and director of the Office of Religious and Spiritual Life, offered another suggestion. They proposed an opportunity to deepen spiritual practices of connection. The message to the students was profound.

> If we strive to transform our collective isolation into an opportunity for communal solitude, we might discover that it is, as it has always been, the seedbed for growth in holiness and wholeness, for communion and connection, for resistance and renewal.
>
> In the suddenly altered pace of our lives, we might discover the stillness we all crave, the stillness from which all true wisdom and justice issue. What we love rather than what we fear may come into sharper focus—and just in time.[23]

Similar sentiments from spiritual and community leaders gave us options and hope that even a communal dark night of the soul could be a source of renewal. Claire Greenwood offered suggestions as to how we could utilize our spiritual resources during a time of great suffering. She wrote,

> The months to come will undoubtedly bring pain, suffering, and fear. My wish to you, gentle readers, is a recognition that "things should not be another way." This is all the stuff of human existence. It's beautiful and traumatizing and it's life. Additionally, I invite you to open up to your surroundings and to your community. This can be a time to get to know neighbors, care for the most vulnerable, share resources, and build connections.
>
> If we can convert our individual suffering and fear into compassion for others, we will suffer less. This is because you and I are not separate. We breathe the same air and touch the same subway poles. As COVID-19 spreads, fear and grief are perhaps inevitable, but so is connection and care. We are all of these things.[24]

23. Kerry Maloney, "Spiritual Resources During the COVID-19 Pandemic," *Harvard Divinity School*, August 17, 2020, https://hds.harvard.edu/life-at-hds/religious-and-spiritual-life/spiritual-resources-during-covid-19-pandemic.

24. Gesshin Claire Greenwood, "Spiritual Advice for Fears of Pandemic," *Tricycle*, March 13, 2020, https://tricycle.org/trikedaily/coronavirus-meditations/?#gesshinclairegreenwood.

History is a reminder that pandemics kill, but they also unsettle fragile social experiments that purport to embrace diversity.

> The last major pandemic, in 1918, was followed by race riots and massacres in 38 cities in 1919, now known as the Red Summer. . . . It's easy to see a parallel between then and now. Many point to potential positive outcomes from what the COVID-19 pandemic and this year's global protests against police violence have exposed. But there should be caution along with the optimism and action. After the Red Summer came the Black Wall Street massacre and other forms of retribution: the passing of the Johnson-Reed Act of 1924, which banned Chinese immigration and imposed immigration quotas, and the rise of the Ku Klux Klan.[25]

It seems that our deepest animosities surface when we are facing our deepest fears.

The Pandemic of Racism

BEFORE WE COULD recover from one national health crisis, another was televised around the world: racism. On May 25, 2020, a Minneapolis police officer kneeled on George Floyd's neck until he was dead. Shock and stillness settled over all of us as 8 minutes and 46 seconds ticked by.[26] Was this a moment of crisis contemplation, experienced by the entire world? Pleas to let him breathe were ignored. As the incident unfolded, phrases from a

---

25. Paul Rucker, as quoted in "How Have Artists Shaped Previous Protest Movements? 7 Historians on How the Past Can Help Us Understand the Present," *Artnet News*, June 16, 2020, https://news.artnet.com/art-world/art-and-protest-historian-response-1882494.

26. Although the time 8:46 became a rallying cry during the protests, authorities contest it. In combining videos of security cameras and bystanders, they find the numbers vary from 7:46 to more than nine minutes. "'It makes no difference,' said Jamar Nelson, who works with the families of crime victims in Minneapolis. 'The bottom line is, it was long enough to kill him, long enough to execute him.'" Nicholas Bogel-Burroughs, "8 Minutes, 46 Seconds Became a Symbol in George Floyd's Death. The Exact Time is Less Clear," *The New York Times*, June 18, 2020, https://www.nytimes.com/2020/06/18/us/george-floyd-timing.html#.

song I taught kindergarteners years ago kept running through my mind: "and if some day you lose your way . . . go up to the kind policeman, the very first one you see." We could not unsee the cruelty. We could not admit our collective responsibility, although we all knew the truth: Police do not respond to black and brown bodies in the same way as they respond to "white"[27] bodies. Yet, we continued the public pretense that we all have equal protection under the law. That fiction cost George Floyd his life.

The real crisis during a viral pandemic and the proliferation of structural racism is that, as a nation, Americans refuse to face reality. Who are we when productivity no longer defines our lives? Whose lives matter when elderly and black, Indigenous, and people of color (BIPOC) folks are more vulnerable to disease? It is important to note that the virus exposed a national vulnerability that is structural, social, and spiritual. Our weaknesses include poverty, pre-existing conditions exacerbated by poor healthcare, substandard and overcrowded housing, and low-paying, high-risk jobs.

But the true crisis in America is diminished compassion for others. We have allowed the top 10 percent to determine the rhythm of our lives. As a consequence, we choose a type of exclusionary patriotism over freedom, enslavement to market forces rather than exploration of our calling and gifts. We harm one another and our environment because we cannot honor the s(S)pirit that enlivens everyone and everything and respects our differences. I believe that we still have a unique opportunity to change everything, including our destructive patterns of behavior. There is so much potential, even as we face new crises.

A crisis forces those caught in its clutches to come to terms with the fact that life as we knew it may never be the same. When the crisis strikes, the response from the village must be a pause. There is little that we can *do*, but we can *be*. We can listen. We can love our neighbors, and we can host the s(S)pirit that flutters over every dawning day. The next chapter discusses this unique form of contemplation.

---

27. "white" is a category of power, privilege, and protection that has nothing to do with race or identity. There is only one human race with many ethnicities and cultures.

Summary

IN THIS CHAPTER, I have addressed the crises that affect communities: natural disasters, pandemics, violent oppression, systemic dehumanization, othering, and microaggressions that destroy health and wellbeing. There are more, but this is intended to be a small book.

As a spiritual teacher, I spend a lot of time speaking to large groups about these realities. I always have the sense that there is not only resistance to the facts, but a desire to get past these realities as quickly as we reasonably can. Often, exemplars are selected to prove the fact that "stuff happened," but everybody landed on their feet.

The fact that the oppressed inevitably arise is not proof that the story has a happy ending. The fact that a few talented BIPOC have succeeded is not an indicator of progress. The fact that Native Americans are reclaiming their culture does not mitigate the harm done. For healing to be declared, we must acknowledge that we have been complicit, silent, and blind to the harm being done to our neighbors.

In the months preceding the pandemic, mass shootings at schools and in public places peaked, and Greta Thunberg, a very young prophet from Sweden, warned the "powers that be" that a new order was rising, that global warming threated life as we know it, and that this rising generation would no longer tolerate the lies and inaction of the elder generations.

Her message struck a note of truth that reverberated throughout global communities, for we all know that we have created a social order where ultimate power lies in the hands of a few and misrepresentation of the truth prevails. The battles between political parties are no longer genteel disagreements, but blood-sport clashes where anything goes. We only look at the news with which we agree—and that, in and of itself, is a crisis.

Our history books no longer teach a long and documented struggle for fairness and justice. Instead, we cling to America's myth of national "goodness" and offer revised versions of history that expunge from our collective memory any evidence of hatred and harm to others.

In the midst of what sometimes seems like collective madness, I still have hope, but it is a "woke" hope with eyes wide open. Despite all evidence to the contrary, I insist on seeing our current state of affairs as the rupture of one state of being that will prepare us for another reality.

Crisis

Spiritual Practices

1. Breathe deeply and exhale slowly three times.
2. Your ancestors survived many crises. What were the crises of their days that required a communal response?
3. What is the crisis of your day that requires a communal response?
4. Sit for ten minutes. Feel the "troubles of this world." Breathe deeply, exhaling your sense of helplessness, inhaling Ella Baker's strength, channeling Rosa Parks' quiet resolve. (Substitute exemplars as needed, but include one exemplar from a cultural community that is not your own.)
5. Remember an instance of oppression against a group that is not yours.
    a. What, if anything, did you feel called to do as an ally? Did you do it? If you did something in response to the crisis, what did you do and what happened as a result?
    b. Do you belong to a community that is currently in crisis? If so, what is happening? Tell the story of what is happening in the voice of a survivor (i.e., "Most of us were women holding children. We were lined up at the border when the Border Patrol approached us and began snatching our babies out of our arms.").
    c. If your community were under siege, what help would you need or want?
6. Read Ibram X. Kendi's *How to Be an Antiracist.* Reflect on and discuss one thing that surprised you and one idea from the book that disturbed you.

Practices Related to Nature and the Environment

1. Have you experienced a natural disaster? Describe the crisis and your community's response.
2. Consider the hurricane disasters in New Orleans or Puerto Rico, and the people stranded and dying without help, food, water, or rescue. What does it mean to be a neighbor during such times?
3. Watch "Three Seconds," a *Film4Climate* First Prize-winning short film: https://vimeo.com/208145716. As you listen, substitute the word "humankind" whenever references to "mankind" are made.

Consider and discuss the message.

4. Native protectors of water have stood up to oil companies and the US government. In years past, activists blocked the destruction of America's redwood trees with their bodies. Describe a crisis that requires immediate action and what actions you might take.

5. How does your community relate and respond to local environmental crises?

6. Take a walk and listen to the songs of the birds and the story of the trees. What do you hear? Write a paragraph describing your reactions to Brian Swimme's idea of the "unseen shaping."

Practices Related to the Pandemic

1. Experience this spiritual practice by Thich Nhat Hanh.[28]

    a. Breathing in, I experience calm in me. Breathing out, I smile to the calm in me.

    b. Breathing in, I experience joy in me. Breathing out, I smile to the joy in me.

    c. Breathing in, I experience equanimity in me. Breathing out, I smile to the equanimity in me.

    d. Breathing in, I experience openness in me. Breathing out, I smile to the openness in me.

    e. Breathing in, I experience happiness in me. Breathing out, I smile to the happiness in me.

2. Ask the Virus: Create a scenario where you are about to meet a virus. Put on your personal protective equipment. Place a chair at the front of the room. The virus can't be seen, so direct your questions to the empty chair. Ask the virus why it's here and how long it plans to stay. What does it say? What other questions might you ask? What responses do you get?[29]

---

28. Thich Nhat Hanh, "Nourishing Positive Emotions," excerpt from *Creating True Peace: Ending Violence in Yourself, Your Family, Your Community, and the World* (New York: Atria, 2003) in *Spirituality and Practice*, https://www.spiritualityand-practice.com/practices/practices/view/26868/nourishing-positive-emotions.

29. This exercise is inspired by Bayo Akomolafe, "I, Coronavirus. Mother. Monster. Activist." *BayoAkomolafe*, April 7, 2020, https://bayoakomolafe.net/project/i-coro-navirus-mother-monster-activist/.

The times are urgent;
let us slow down.

—Traditional African wisdom saying

Slowing down is . . . about lingering in the places we
are not used to. Seeking out new questions. Becoming
accountable to more than what rests on the surface.
Seeking roots. Slowing down is taking care of ghosts,
hugging monsters, sharing silence, embracing the
weird. . . . The idea of slowing down is not about
getting answers, it is about questioning our
questions. It is about staying in the
places that are haunted.

—Bayo Akomolafe, "A Slower Urgency:
We Will Dance with Mountains"

CHAPTER TWO

CONTEMPLATION

A contemplative is one who takes the time to observe herself and the world around her closely and sensitively, with openness and without an agenda. He observes his own thoughts and feelings and patterns of behavior. She actively observes herself, others, the plants, the animals, the wind, the rain, the streams and rivers. Contemplation honors the world with open, undivided attention.[1]

Slowing Down

THIS BOOK CONSIDERS a type of contemplation that arises out of crisis. I am referring to a state of devastation brought on by ecological and natural causes, as well as injustice and the oppression of a group of people. These are not circumstances that invite or induce contemplation in its ordinary practice. Yet, Bayo Akomolafe suggests that

---

1. John Crockett, "Contemplative Ecology: Contemplation for a World in Crisis," *The Natural Contemplative*, www.naturalcontemplative.com/essays/crisis. html.

during a crisis, contemplative slowing is exactly what is needed. He writes that slowing down

> seems like the wrong thing to do when there's fire on the mountain [but] in "hurrying up" all the time, we often lose sight of the abundance of resources that might help us meet today's most challenging crises. We rush through into the same patterns we are used to. Of course, there isn't a single way to respond to crisis; there is no universally correct way. However, the call to slow down works to bring us face to face with the invisible, the hidden, the unremarked, the yet-to-be-resolved.[2]

In the midst of devastating crises, we are asked to do the counterintuitive. When the times call for anxiety, flight, or fight, Akomolafe urges us to slow down, to allow for the possibility of contemplative refuge, respite, and renewal. To slow down and be still is to allow both the source of our troubles and options for recovery to emerge.

Contemplation is a soft word in a hard world. Most of us consider the practice to be a voluntary entry into deep and often sacred reflection, while in safe and comfortable spaces. Sitting in stillness allows a settling of the mind and the spirit. Through breath, our bodies are revived and attuned to divine presence and cosmic connections.

I have always understood contemplation to be a choice for peace and an opportunity to disconnect from the relentless rhythms of work and productivity. However, in its historically understood context, contemplation requires the privilege and time to retreat from the frontlines of everyday life, if only for a little while. For most people of color/culture and communities under siege, such comforts are inconceivable. We dare not shift our gaze for even a moment to consider an alternative reality. Survival requires an alert spiritual and embodied stance. To contemplate (in the ordinary sense of the word) during a crisis might increase the possibility that we miss or misread signs of danger in our immediate environment.

---

2. Bayo Akomolafe, "A Slower Urgency: We Will Dance with Mountains," *Bayo Akomolafe*, https://bayoakomolafe.net/project/a-slower-urgency-we-will-dance-with-mountains/.

We have to be present or "woke" or we might miss the rumbling of a dam that is about to break, a volcano that is about to erupt, or the seething resentment just below the surface of a police officer's polite and routine request for driver's license and registration. We might let our guard down at the wrong moment—with lethal consequences. To be "woke" is to be spiritually alert and willing to be a witness to injustice or catastrophe:

> We owe one another: a witness. When we see systems that hurt and hinder, we owe it to the hindered to train our eyes on their plight. If we are being wronged, we owe it to ourselves and anyone in a similar position to make our voices heard. To be woke is to see and say what has gone unseen, unspoken. We have eyes, voices. We can offer both.[3]

Everyday Contemplation

As I recalled in *Joy Unspeakable*,[4] my childhood included raucous play in the morning, lunch, then shower and a Sit during the afternoon until dinner. During the Sit, my sisters and I could read, write, or just heighten our awareness of the world around us, but stillness and reflection were required. Contemplative porch practices are no longer required of me; they are part of me.

My contemplative practices include writing, music and dancing, prayer, stillness, social justice activism, and teaching. These practices are the choices of one individual. What happens when the practices are communal and practiced together? What happens when contemplation is not a personal practice, but a collective, biogenetic, and spiritual response to crisis?

---

3. Tomi Adeyemi, "What Does It Take to Be Woke, Stay Woke, and Live Woke? An Exploration of the Definition—and Weight—of the Word," *O: The Oprah Magazine*, February 6, 2019, https://www.oprahmag.com/life/relationships-love/a26145644/woke-definition/. As far back as 1962, *The New York Times* published an essay on appropriation of Black culture, "If You're Woke You Dig It," by William Melvin Kelley, an African American novelist known in some quarters as the godfather of "woke." Then, in 1972, a play written about Jamaican activist Marcus Garvey by Barry Beckham, *Garvey Lives!* contained the stirring line: "I been sleeping all my life. And now that Mr. Garvey done woke me up, I'm gon' stay woke."

4. Barbara Holmes, *Joy Unspeakable: Contemplative Practices of the Black Church* (Minneapolis: Augsburg Fortress, 2004).

Contemplation is the highest expression of [human] intellectual and spiritual life. . . . It is spiritual wonder. It is spontaneous awe at the sacredness of life, of being. . . . It is a vivid realization of the fact that life and being in us proceed from an invisible, transcendent and infinitely abundant source. Contemplation is, above all, awareness of the reality of that Source.[5]

Thomas Merton (1915–1968) reassured us that when we reach the limits of our knowledge categories and intuitions, there is a wellspring, deep and inexhaustible. In the darkness, we can gather in Spirit and be filled by this Source.

Contemplation is not just an effective response to crisis. It can also arise during the most intense aspects of the event. When bodies are being tortured, when minds are pushed to the breaking point, the human spirit falls through the cracks of the crisis into the center of contemplation. Howard Thurman (1899–1981) referred to this inner space as an island, a place that cannot be breached without personal consent: "When all hope for release in the world seems unrealistic and groundless, the heart turns to a way of escape beyond the present order."[6]

When the ordinary isn't ordinary anymore and the crisis is upon us, the self can center in this refuge that I am calling "crisis contemplation," a space that is neither the result of spiritual seeking nor the voluntary entry into meditative spaces. It is a cracking open, the rupture and shattering of self, community, expectations, and presumptions about how the world works. It is the result of trauma, freefall, and wounding.

As a result of the precipitating event, the group experiences shock, shattering, silencing of reason, ineffability, and waiting. We may not have a choice about experiencing the crisis, but in community we do have choices about how we will survive. As a Black woman of color and culture, I have chosen to survive as a contemplative, seeking the solace of practices that remind me of my childhood and my connections to the source of all being.

---

5. Thomas Merton, *New Seeds of Contemplation* (New York: New Directions, 1961), 1.

6. Howard Thurman, *Deep River and The Negro Spiritual Speaks of Life and Death* (Richmond, IN: Friends United, 1975), 29.

Contemplation after or during crisis is a stillness in the aftermath of a primal scream, the abyss of unknowing, and the necessity of surviving the trauma together. Perhaps our definitions of "contemplation" need adjustment to reflect our unique social locations and inward journeys. As it turns out, there are many entry points into these sacred reflective spaces.

I can enter alone or with my community. We can journey inward, with or without music, with our bodies as engaged as our minds, but we must relinquish control and seek grounding within the mystical depths of inner spaces.

> The hardest thing to let go of is the idea of spiritual attainment, specifically enlightenment itself. . . . The ego's games and desires must be exhausted before any kind of "finding" or "door opening" will happen.[7]

When a crisis of spirit or soul is visited upon a community as a result of oppression, genocide, disease, or natural disasters, an entire community can tumble through torn social safety nets into stillness. The contemplation that results is a freefall from what we thought we knew, to a new story that is being written by events and experiences that we cannot control.

We cannot save ourselves from what is happening. All we can do is breathe and survive. Often, we find ourselves in a place of situational refuge in the midst of a disordered world. There is nothing to do but let go of our personal and collective sense of normalcy.

While the bombs are falling over Hiroshima and Nagasaki, as your Hutu neighbors are murdering your Tutsi family members in Rwanda, while you are tight-packed in the hold of a slave ship, there is no choice. No words of prayer or cries for help will change your circumstances. At the moment of crisis, you grasp one another spiritually, gather your collective courage, and let go!

---

7. Jessica Davidson, "How to Survive a Dark Night of the Soul," *Jessica Davidson*, June 23, 2014, https://jessicadavidson.co.uk/2014/06/23/how-to-survive-a-dark-night-of-the-soul/.

Letting Go

When I let go of what I am
I become what I might be.
   —John Heider

THE STORIES WE tell ourselves about who we are and how we arrived at a certain point in history are entertaining and they help to organize the worlds that we create, but ultimately they have nothing to do with reality. A crisis can plummet a community into spaces where nothing can be known and everything is on hold. I am referring to the shock that results from a sudden lack of order, norms, shared values, and story.

When, without warning, neighbors become genocidal enemies, reliance on a weak social order must be supplanted by transitions from one reality to another. Those transitions can only take place if we are willing to let go of what we have known, the worlds we have created, and our assumptions about "how things are." To let go is the precursor to being reborn. We discard the baggage of societal expectations and, like a morning glory, open to the possibilities of each new day, each new moment, even if those possibilities are shadowy and disorientating.

Unfortunately, in the West, we don't let go of anything. We hold onto reputation and material goods long after they are no longer needed. We store acquired stuff in every nook and household cranny before renting a storage unit so that we can continue to hold onto our stuff. Dazed, we clutch at relationships long after they are on life support and cling to a past that no longer exists, grasping, desperate, and confused.

We say that we are letting go, but, in our society, letting go is more like a tug of war. We diligently guard our stories (true or not), our lifestyles, and our belief systems until they are ripped from our sweaty palms. And yet, letting go is a necessary part of transformation.

Given the fact that crisis contemplation only takes place under extreme circumstances, letting go may be the only path toward rebirth. The truth of the matter is that we are clutching at nothing! The stripping has already begun. When the worst happens, our addictive desire for control and the futility of our desires are fully exposed. If we are wise, we open our minds, our hands, and our hearts, and let go.

However, I do not want to mislead you: Letting go has consequences. Finally, the striving is over, the effort to salvage and fix, be or do something, is over. It is as if we have been clinging to the wall of a mountain of our own making, a mountain of expectations, striving, and goals. When that mountain disappears, we plummet.

Perhaps your team is within one or two steps of the summit when it happens. The deportation orders are on the kitchen table. You and your neighbors have lived in North America for decades, or you were brought here as children. Now you are being sent back to your country of origin, away from your family. You realize that you are not alone, because ICE raids your neighborhood every few weeks, but this crisis is of such magnitude that it will take more than resistance and political intervention. Much more is needed that you cannot provide. And so, you let go of the fear.

When we let go, the only constants are God's love and God's promise that we will never be left alone. We let go of our public persona, our striving and pursuits. Sometimes it takes a crisis to remind us that we are not in control. This space that I name contemplative is a place of breaking, relinquishment, and waiting. This is not occurring in peaceful repose on our meditation pillows, not during the shared experiences of village life, but in the midst of a disorienting freefall.

The Collective Freefall

It happens so slowly,
it happens so suddenly,
it is safe and then it is not.

When it happens,
we are certain
about everything,

and then the fall
strips us of knowing
and doing,

and leaves us with
being.

Together we fall,
sweaty, shattered,
and gulping the darkness.

I AM EXPLORING CRISIS contemplation in a communal context. The contemplation that follows a crisis is experienced as a freefall from a shared and collective consciousness into emptiness that is "immeasurable and indescribable, . . . [a space that] knows no conflict. It knows no separation. It knows only love and acceptance. Inner emptiness is absolutely inclusive. That is its nature."[8] As the crisis peaks, we enter a space of belonging that steadies our fears and our faith.

The contemplative moments that follow do not rely upon a fixed sense of self and society. Instead, there is a sense of fluidity to our collective purpose and consciousness. Nicki Lisa Cole quotes Émile Durkheim (1858–1917) in describing collective consciousness this way.

> Collective consciousness is something "common to the whole of society." . . . It is not an individual condition or phenomenon, but a social one. As a social phenomenon, it is "diffused across society as a whole," and "has a life of its own." It is through collective consciousness that values, beliefs, and traditions can be passed down through generations. Though individual people live and die, this collection of intangible things, including the social norms connected to them, are cemented in our social institutions and thus exist independent of individual people.[9]

Jesuit priest Pierre Teilhard de Chardin (1881–1955) wrote of collective consciousness as a layer of awareness that envelops the earth.[10] He

---

8. Crockett.

9. Nicki Lisa Cole, "The Concept of Collective Consciousness: What It Is and How It Holds Society Together," *ThoughtCo.com*, January 16, 2019, https://www.thoughtco.com/collective-consciousness-definition-3026118.

10. Pierre Teilhard de Chardin, *The Phenomenon of Man* (New York: Harper & Row, 1961), 244.

called this membrane the "noosphere" (from the Greek *nous,* meaning "mind"), a term first coined by Vladimir Vernadsky (1863–1945). The noosphere is the collective consciousness of humanity, the networks of thought and emotion in which all are immersed.[11]

> The evolving noosphere [sphere of human thought] . . . calls for a collective spirituality, one in which people, individually and collectively, create and contribute to its evolution. The purpose of such a relational spirituality is to bring the noosphere to its highest level of convergence, eventually operating as a single consciousness. This convergent oneness of humanity and the planet will be a knowledge-based and love-inspired union and communion. Only in this collective way may we create an adequate infrastructure for the full emergence of Christ as a Cosmic Christ (1 Cor 6:15, 17, 19). In this perspective, when Jesus says, "The Kingdom of God is among you" [Luke 17:21], it would mean, in Teilhard's language, that the divine project is already under way.[12]

This view of Earth reveals a cosmological oneness that may be the foundation of life on this planet. In an effort to inspire competitiveness, undergird market forces, and stoke national loyalties, we have obscured the multi-dimensional aspects of reality and the probability that unity is part of the natural order. When we finally let go and accept the freefall, everything changes.

> Go deeply enough into these dark parts of yourself until you feel your resistance letting go, struggle being replaced by surrender, tension turning into relaxation, fear giving way to an awareness that there is nothing to fear.[13]

---

11. Chardin, 278.

12. Louis M. Savary, *The New Spiritual Exercises: In the Spirit of Pierre Teilhard de Chardin* (Mahwah, NJ: Paulist, 2010), 27.

13. Lynn Woodland, "The Healing Power of Darkness," *Maya del Mar's Daykeeper Journal,* December 2013, https://daykeeperjournal.com/2013/12/healing-power-darkness/.

During crisis contemplation, all the systems that we have put in place to undergird our fantasies collapse and we fall headlong, together, into the power of divine intention and the mystery of an inner and outer cosmos.

In the midst of a collective freefall, there is blessed darkness and an uncomfortably familiar fog that creeps over our state of shock like an enveloping enigma as old as the universe. We have tried, through our religious systems, to avoid this. We have glorified the light, made sacrifices to its heat, and yet, it is the darkness that welcomes us when we finally let go.

> It is alright to stop striving.
> It is alright to grieve losses and then let go.
> It is alright to withdraw from ordinary pursuits for a while.
> It is alright to get out of the driver's seat and sit in the back for a while.
> It is alright to let the Spirit lead.

Hello Darkness, My Old Friend

Only in the darkness can you see the stars.
—Martin Luther King, Jr.

Into the darkness they go, the wise and the lovely.
—Edna St. Vincent Millay

As a CHILD, I feared darkness. I don't know how to locate the source of this aversion, since the only darkness that I knew nurtured, birthed, and comforted me. As an African American woman, I wear darkness as a skin color that I love. It is a reminder of African origins, hidden in my genes, but not accessible through memory. Without darkness, I would not be! I entered the world from the nurturing darkness of the womb and relied upon a dark and resourceful family, community, and cosmos for my well-being.

As I came of age, in the midst of a family of women mystics, I began to interpret their mysteries as spaces for travel: dark, but not foreboding; thick, but lit by their discernment. In this realm, my Aunties would encounter those being born and those transitioning to the other side.

From their wisdom, I learned that darkness in dreamscapes is shadowed and starlit. We come from the darkness and return to it.

But there are many types of darkness. There is the darkness of determined ignorance and hatred, impenetrable and smothering. There is the tiny microcosm of darkness that gave birth to the universe, its new realities and new worlds. There is the mothering darkness of the womb, and the protective darkness of the "cloud by night."

> *In the beginning there is natal*
> *darkness, it is the womb out of*
> *which we are born.*
> *It is the rich loam, feeding and*
> *strengthening us,*
> *encouraging us to put forth*
> *deep roots. It makes no difference*
> *whether we are tiny seeds or*
> *majestic redwoods,*
> *we grow toward the light fed*
> *by the darkness.*

Because I saw my Aunties negotiate darkness as a reality with as much potential as light, I stopped being afraid of the dark. I realized that sight and insight were not dependent upon the glaring light produced by humans, for there was an inner light that glowed and revealed much more. Without really trying, I could close the curtains of my eyelids and see with greater clarity than with my eyes open.

And so it is for infants who are born with a veil or thin membrane over their faces, a sign to the midwives and mystics that the child will see beyond the earthly realm into a multi-layered spirit realm. Those who show such inclinations are groomed and mentored in the ways of African diasporan mysticism.

In this way, I became aware that the familiar world was permeable and Spirit-soaked. A fascinating state of affairs, and yet, none of my elders would tolerate or accept bizarre behavior as proof of power or mystical gifts. Elders could determine the difference between folks with special needs and mental health issues from those with spiritual ties to other realms. No matter how many gifts children seemed to have, parents insisted that childhood continue in ordinary ways. And so, gifts of the spirit had to be integrated into everyday practices in order to be acknowledged as part of family and community life.

Accordingly, my siblings and I learned to listen deeply to grownups talking about the warnings and news from ancestors on the other side. We welcomed both darkness and light, stoked wonder by scanning night skies, and nurtured the seeds of contemplation during long afternoon sojourns on the front porch. Protected from the difficulties of the world, we could take deep dives into contemplative spaces as we grappled with issues of identity.

I knew who I was, but would struggle to determine where I fit into the life of the community. My mirror captured the reflection of a brown-skinned girl with bright eyes and a happy smile. Racism, colorism, and rejection because of the color of my skin would come later, when I realized that some members of "white" society considered me to be a diminished human being, a second-class citizen, an object of hatred and random violence.

My reaction to this reality was surprise. I was surprised that dominant culture had no knowledge of the joy in our communities, families, and churches. BIPOC safety required that we become very knowledgeable about how white communities operated, but they knew very little about us. One thing was certain: I knew that I lived with resourceful, kind, and mystical people. I felt sorry for people who hated our gorgeous skin colors, yet tanned themselves like leather to achieve a similar effect.

I would ask my father, a psychiatric social worker with a Jungian inclination, why the haters were so weird. Anyone with any sense knew that life was about energy. If you hate anyone for any reason, you are wasting life energy that you might really need at some point. My dad would nod and say, "It's their baggage; let them carry it. Focus on using the gifts that God gave you to help people." And so I did. Without realizing it, I was learning the lesson that logic and reason were not the only, or even the best, tools for negotiating life. A healthy dose of conjure and improvisation could act as a balm for the chaos.

It wasn't until religion was introduced into my early life, with its dark and light associations with good and evil, that the confusion was compounded. I had questions, but nothing could change my mind about the creative potential of my own dark self and the love of a God who "dwelled in deep darkness."[14] In my mind, church talk about an association of darkness with evil and goodness with light made no sense. I knew that darkness held and healed me. So, there had to be many types of darkness that I could differentiate, dismiss, or embrace.

> Surely the darkness shall cover me,
> and the light around me become night . . .
> the darkness and light are both alike to You.
> —Psalm 139:11–12

Thank goodness for the darkness that blankets our freefall through the crisis and into the rich loam of contemplative potential. I am grateful that when we are at our lowest point, a portal opens that beckons us toward healing and restoration. In the midst of crisis, we are given the opportunity to shed simplified versions of reality for multi-dimensional and mystical spaces.

In the blessed darkness, we watch our dreams of conformity morph into a complexity that transforms us together. When crisis breaks us open, we plummet into a contemplative space that does not rely on our effort, but strengthens our collective desire to grow toward God together.

Experiencing Crisis Contemplation

I OFFER HERE A few examples of how crisis contemplation might be experienced. There is a sense of ineffability that follows the rupture, letting go, freefall, and darkness. Words are useless, will not come to mind, and—even if available—would be of no use. Since the context for the crisis is communal, those in the midst of despair want to feel the comfort and presence of those around them, and yet their circumstances will not allow them to communicate in the usual ways. I suggest a few key factors

14. References to God's dwelling place in a dark cloud or using darkness as a covering and canopy are found in 2 Chronicles 6:1–2, Exodus 20:21, 1 Kings 8:12, and Psalm 18:11.

that may arise during crisis contemplation: the eclipse, the moan, and the stillness.

The Eclipse

There is no chance that we will fall apart
There is no chance
There are no parts.

—June Jordan, "Poem Number Two on Bell's Theorem,
or The New Physicality of Long Distance Love"

In her clear "everyday" voice, poet June Jordan (1936–2002) affirmed the wholeness of everything as a reliable platform of reality. No matter how fractured things seem to be, no matter how the crisis splinters our delusions, there is a solid foundation within and beneath us, beside and between us. We can depend on this wholeness when it is experienced as a dark night of the soul for individuals, or an eclipse of the ordinary for the community.

An eclipse occurs when one object gets in between us and another object and blocks our view. From Earth, we routinely experience two kinds of eclipses: an eclipse of the moon and an eclipse of the sun.[15] Of course, the scientific explanation is more detailed and comprehensive, but, for our purposes, what matters most about an eclipse is the sense of temporary absence. We are not permanently blocked from the light. Also, we are not able to rely upon our sight to overcome the obstruction.

Finally, during an eclipse, we have a dimming of the familiar and a loss of taken-for-granted clues that we rely upon every day to remind us of who we are and why we are here. Yet, although we are not always comfortable in darkness, the invitation to come away from life in the spotlight is intriguing. Could there be a blessing in the shadows?

---

15. The term "eclipse" is derived from the Latin *eclipsis*, which itself is derived from Greek *ekleipsis*, meaning "an abandonment," literally "a failing, forsaking," from *ekleipein*, "to forsake a usual place, fail to appear, be eclipsed." During a solar eclipse, the sun isn't actually "abandoning" or "forsaking" us; what causes the darkness is that we are in the shadow of the moon. For more, see "What Is an Eclipse?" *NASA*, May 3, 2017, https://www.nasa.gov/audience/forstudents/5-8/features/nasa-knows/what-is-an-eclipse-58.

The eclipse reminds us to linger in the darkness, to savor the silence, to embrace the shadow—for the light is coming, the resurrection is afoot, transformation is unfolding, for God is working in secret and in silence to create us anew.[16]

This renewal will require a rebirthing.

The Moan

In *Joy Unspeakable*, I rely upon the research of James Noel[17] (1948–2016) and my own Middle Passage studies to form a theory about village formation. Noel argued, and I agree, that the moan is the utterance that communicates the ineffability of the crisis, the need to connect to others nearby, and our dependence on a groaning Holy Spirit.

We moan to give birth,
to traverse non-linear time,
and to signal movement from
one state of being to another.
We moan as a sign of life,
to give notice to spiritual
bystanders that what looks
like an ending is actually a
beginning.

In similar fashion, the Holy Spirit groans the prayers for us that we cannot utter while the crisis continues. In the Epistle to the Romans (8:26–27) the Apostle Paul states:

In the same way, the Spirit helps us in our weakness. We do not know what we ought to pray for, but the Spirit . . . intercedes for us through wordless groans.

16. Linda Anderson-Little, "Embracing Darkness and the Solar Eclipse," *SoulStory-Writer*, August 22, 2017, https://www.soulstorywriter.net/109-embracing-darkness-the-solar-eclipse.

17. James A. Noel, "Call and Response: The Meaning of the Moan and Significance of the Shout in Black Worship," *Reformed Liturgy & Music* 28, no. 2 (Spring 1994): 72–76.

Throughout chapter 8 in Romans, Paul writes of the sacred utterances of creation and humankind in crisis. We don't know what will emerge from this time of tarrying, but we do know that something is being born. Like a woman in labor, there is expectation in the darkness, anticipation amid the suffering, hope permeating the pain. Something new is being born and something old is being transformed.

Stillness

In the stillness of quiet, if we listen, we can hear the whisper of the heart giving strength to weakness, courage to fear, hope to despair.

—Howard Thurman

Silence is helpful, but you don't need it in order to find stillness. Even when there is noise, you can be aware of the stillness underneath the noise, of the space in which the noise arises. That is the inner space of pure awareness, consciousness itself.

—Eckhart Tolle

After the eclipse and the moan comes the stillness. Stillness and silence are not the same. One can be enfolded into the other in ways that enhance the benefits of both, yet they are not the same. Stillness is a state of wholeness, an antidote to the fragmentation of BIPOC people that comes with marginalization. "When we are fragmented, [we are] lost from ourselves, our culture, our people, our communities, the earth, our light, [our shadows and our darkness,] from God and our 'spiritness.'"[18] In the midst of crisis, there is fragmentation and wounding. Sitting in stillness may allow the pieces of us to reassemble. But sometimes, the crisis is so devastating that the healing requires drumming and song, chanting and ritual, not just once, but often. There is stillness in the midst of it all.

---

18. Shelly P. Harrell, Shena Young, and Thema Bryant-Davis, "African-Centered Cultural Considerations for Contemplative Practices: Mindfulness, Meditation, and Yoga," presentation to the 50th Annual Convention of the Association of Black Psychologists, June 30, 2018, Oakland, CA, slide 5, https://www.slideshare.net/Shelly Harrell/africancentered-cultural-considerations-for-contemplative-practices-ce-symposium.

I close this chapter with a meditation on stillness written by Eckhart Tolle:

We have forgotten what rocks, plants, and animals still know. We have forgotten how to *be*—to be still, to be ourselves, to be where life is: Here and Now.

Whenever you bring your attention to anything natural, anything that has come into existence without human intervention, you step out of the prison of conceptualized thinking and, to some extent, participate in the state of connectedness with Being in which everything natural still exists.

To bring your attention to a stone, a tree, or an animal does not mean to *think* about it, but simply to perceive it, to hold it in your awareness.

Something of its essence then transmits itself to you. You can sense how still it is, and in doing so the same stillness arises within you. You sense how deeply it rests in Being—completely at one with what it is and where it is. In realizing this, you too come to a place of rest deep within yourself.[19]

Summary

As it turns out, contemplation that arises from a crisis or collective trauma is a displacement of everyday life and a freefall into "what comes next." As the crisis sweeps away our former life together, our arrogance and fantasies, all we can do is reflect on the memories of another and more tranquil existence, and accustom ourselves to a new and welcoming darkness.

The darkness to which I refer is not a space of fear. It is an involuntary centering in a reality that is not always available to us when our egos are lit. Crises open portals of a deeper knowing. When the crisis occurs, the only way out is through, so we take a cue from nature and relax into the stillness, depending upon one another and the breath of life!

19. Eckhart Tolle, *Stillness Speaks* (Novato, CA: New World Library, 2003), 77–79.

Spiritual Practices

1. Sit in a darkened room. Find and feel the warmth and friendliness of its embrace. Welcome stillness as you sit and give thanks for the darkness that nurtures us. Then, as you come out of the depths of solace, list the blessings of darkness for you and your community.

2. Name a time of eclipse for your community. What happened and how did you respond?

3. Reflect on these two paragraphs:

    "One of the great surprises on the human journey is that we come to full consciousness precisely by shadowboxing, facing our own contradictions, and making friends with our own mistakes and failings. People who have had no inner struggles are invariably superficial and uninteresting. We tend to endure them more than appreciate them because they have little to communicate and show little curiosity."[20]

    In the words of Fr. Richard Rohr, "Shadow work is what I call 'falling upward.' Lady Julian of Norwich (1342–1416) put it best of all: 'First there is the fall, and then we recover from the fall. And both are the mercy of God!' God hid holiness quite well: the proud will never recognize it, and the humble will fall into it every day—not even realizing it is holiness."[21]

4. Ask yourself the following questions about your shadows: What are you hiding—what fears, weaknesses? What do you want to shed?

5. Name examples of shadows in one of your communities. How do shadows help or hurt the work of reconciliation?

Practices Related to Nature and the Environment

Open your window, feel the fresh air, sit and listen to the sounds of nature.

---

20. Richard Rohr, "Shadowboxing," *Center for Action and Contemplation*, September 8, 2019, https://cac.org/shadowboxing-2019-09-08/.

21. Rohr, "Shadowboxing." Fr. Rohr's paraphrase of Julian of Norwich, *Revelations of Divine Love*, Long Text, chapter 61.

Sit until the fog burns off. . . .

Sit until the sun completely sets. . . . Sit until the rain ends . . . or begins. . . .

Watch an animal, even an insect at work or play until it departs. . . .

Sit until the puddle dries in the sun. . . .

Sit and watch a shadow until it has crossed your path. . . .

Sit until the birds finish their song. . . .

If you can, sit beneath a tree until it lets go of a leaf and you see (or even hear) it fall to the ground.

If you can, sit at a lake and watch the surface until the wind shifts or stops. . . .

Or simply sit until that cloud completely changes shape, and disappears or passes on the horizon. . . .[22]

The Moaning Meditation

Form a small circle or circles (10–15 circle mates are enough). Hold hands to round the circle. Step in closely, then turn your back to the center of the circle and face outward. Decide whether you will start rocking together toward left or right, then begin your rocking movements as if you are in the hold of a ship. Start to moan. Continue until you reach a natural stopping point. Leave the circle and sit for ten more minutes in silence. Discuss your experience.

22. Christopher Willard, "Two Simple Mindfulness Practices to Help You Connect with Nature: Celebrate Earth Day by Tuning In to the Rhythms of the Earth," *Mindful*, April 22, 2020, https://www.mindful.org/two-simple-mindfulness-practices-to-help-you-connect-with-nature/.

But all our phrasing—race relations, racial chasm, racial justice, racial profiling, white privilege, even white supremacy—serves to obscure that racism is a visceral experience, that it dislodges brains, blocks airways, rips muscle, extracts organs, cracks bones, breaks teeth. You must never look away from this. You must always remember that the sociology, the history, the economics, the graphs, the charts, the regressions all land, with great violence, upon the body.

—Ta-Nehisi Coates,
Between the World and Me

CHAPTER THREE

WOUNDS

Wounds inflicted upon the village pierce the self and soul of us, shatter the I and we of us. We have seen it before, so many times, and yet we are surprised, and unwilling to look into the vacant gaze of systems that decapitate, mutilate, and incarcerate.

We can stop them, you know. It won't be easy, but it can be done. All we have to do is redirect our resources and repent for the harm that systems have done on our behalf.

We can testify and record with our phones, a sacred and necessary witness, and we can go get the monsters that we have unleashed!

T A-NEHISI COATES REMINDS us that systemic racism is not just a theory, a discussion topic, or an abstract idea. It is a violent and aggressive reality that crushes bodies and destroys lives. "Racial oppression is a traumatic form of interpersonal violence which can lacerate the spirit, scar the soul, and puncture the psyche."[1]

---

1. Kenneth V. Hardy, "Healing the Hidden Wounds of Racial Trauma," *Reclaiming Children and Youth*, vol. 22, no. 1 (Spring 2013): 25.

In the African American community, we "say their names" after every public execution as a ritual of remembrance. We march in their honor, attend their funerals, and then repeat the ritual with different names, different circumstances, different police officers, same outcomes. We did not have time to heal from the murder of George Floyd before Malcolm Harsch and Robert Fuller were found hanging from trees in Palmdale, California. With only security camera footage, the murmurs of suicide could not be refuted.

Within that same timeframe, an unarmed intoxicated man, Rayshard Brooks, who fell asleep in a Wendy's drive-thru lane, was killed by Atlanta police. When first encountered, he asked to be allowed to go to his sister's house to sleep it off. During a scuffle, he took the officer's taser and was running away. He was shot in the back multiple times.

It is shocking but true that the incidents keep occurring. The killing of Asian women in Atlantan massage parlors seemed to be yet another incident until the police reported that the murders were not racially motivated. The Asian community and their allies say otherwise. The ethnic/racial groups and circumstances change, but the ultimate outcome is the same: the lives of BIPOC people don't seem to matter.

In this chapter, we address the effects of historical and collective trauma inflicted upon current generations and the epigenetic consequences for generations yet to come. Even if we have not personally experienced a collective crisis, we bear in our bodies the trauma suffered by our ancestors. During the recent viral and racial pandemics, ancestral trauma safely stored in my genes erupted and rose in my throat like bile—an unsettling context for contemplation.

Collective Trauma

Collective trauma is a cataclysmic event that shatters the basic fabric of society. Aside from the horrific loss of life, collective trauma is also a crisis of meaning.[2]

---

2. Gilad Hirschberger, "Collective Trauma and the Social Construction of Meaning," *Frontiers in Psychology* 9:1441 (August 2018), doi: 10.3389/fpsyg.2018.01441.

As an extended community, we saw George Floyd die whether we wanted to or not. Collective trauma is defined as a crisis shared by a group of people of any size, up to and including an entire society. Traumatic events witnessed by an entire society can stir up collective sentiment, often resulting in a shift in that society's identity. Kai Erickson describes in detail the differences between individual and collective trauma:

> By *individual trauma* I mean a blow to the psyche that breaks through one's defenses so suddenly and with such brutal force that one cannot react to it effectively. . . . By *collective trauma* . . . I mean a blow to the basic tissues of social life that damages the bonds attaching people together and impairs the prevailing sense of communality. . . . "We" no longer exist as a connected pair or as linked cells in a larger communal body.[3]

Resmaa Menakem also addresses the issue of collective trauma. He writes, "Trauma and healing aren't just private experiences. Sometimes trauma is a collective experience, in which case our approaches for mending must be collective and communal."[4]

The wounds of BIPOC communities are fresh, historical, intergenerational, and epigenetic. They continue to seep and drain, while phantom trails of fear and despair etch our collective souls.

When we talk about collective wounds today, we no longer refer to single or sequential catastrophic or geographic events that wound a community (i.e., slavery, genocide, etc.). To be wounded, we don't have to be located in the same place at the same time. We can view crises on social media or television at different times and locations, and people of different ethnicities can still experience the collective trauma and wounding of people trapped in racist systems.

If only the harm was seldom. If only the events were as shocking to the perpetrators as to the victims. If only we learned from our mistakes. Instead, the wounds inflicted upon entire societies are historical,

---

3. Kai T. Erikson, *Everything in Its Path: Destruction of Community in the Buffalo Creek Flood* (New York: Simon and Schuster, 1976), 153–154.

4. Resmaa Menakem, *My Grandmother's Hands: Racialized Trauma and the Pathway to Mending Our Hearts and Bodies* (Las Vegas: Central Recovery Press, 2017), chap. 1.

deep, and reoccurring. The infliction of catastrophic harm, as a result of natural or unnatural causes, continues to this day and looms on the horizons of our tomorrows. (I need not list them again. I recited instances of trauma-inducing harm to our communities in the first chapter.)

Wounds inflicted on the community occur because of a willingness to do to others what we wouldn't want to happen to us or ours. But what are the effects in our everyday lives? We know what trauma looks like in the lives of veterans when they return from war with PTSD, but we have only recently acknowledged these same wounds in the lives of BIPOC people living in the Americas.

Where do you turn when everything that you know and rely upon is shattered or withdrawn? What do you do when there is no reasonable hope of human help because everyone in your community is in the same situation, while others, who are not being subjected to harm, are looking the other way? This is the testimony of those subject to racial wounding in their everyday lives:

> "It's constantly a reminder every single day, when you go down the street, when you walk out your house, go to the store," said demonstrator Alicia Wilson. "Eyes are always on you for no reason. That does something to one's psyche. That eats at your soul, when you've done nothing but be alive."
>
> Desmond Campbell says he used to have "a deep fear of ambush." He would hesitate walking around corners, even when he knew he was in a relatively safe neighborhood.
>
> He says going to therapy has helped him learn to stay calm.
>
> "It's a matter of me being in a place now where I don't have to feel like my head is always on a swivel," he said. "Now I have that sense of feeling ambushed under control. It's something you have to constantly work with . . . that's part of the trauma."[5]

---

5. Sammy Caiola, "Black Leaders Are Creating Healing Spaces to Combat the Mental Stress of Racism, Injustice," *CapRadio*, June 18, 2020, https://www.capradio.org/articles/2020/06/18/black-leaders-are-creating-healing-spaces-to-combat-the-mental-stress-of-racism-injustice/.

The wounds of racism manifest in the individual but are not personal. They are inflicted because of the mythologies of race and the structural violence of racism. Ultimately, suffering of the magnitude that I am describing cannot be resolved by individuals.

> There is an aspect of suffering that is not within our rational reach. Pain is a parallel universe that sends shock waves breaking over our consciousness, daring us to succumb. . . . Thus in suffering, we face the loss of our own personal universe.[6]

We also lose all sense of collective purpose and belonging. During such times, the only option is to move toward healing together. No matter how tenuous and invisible the bonds of community may be, individuals must, for their personal and collective safety, work out their survival together.

I am both hopeful that change is on its way, and speechless because of the brazen refusal to treat black and brown bodies as human. My hope does not arise because of the protests, their multi-ethnic cultural makeup, or the *mea culpas* being issued by corporate interests. I am hopeful because no one who saw the casual murder of George Floyd can unsee it, dismiss it, or excuse it. The humanity within each of us has been stirred and awakened.

As I was writing this chapter, ICE was in the midst of raids upon the homes of Mexican and Latin American immigrants in the US. The crisis is personal when immigrants (some who have served in our military) are separated from children and family members, rounded up during terror-inducing raids, and deported, but it is also collective.

It is happening right before our eyes, yet the response of American citizens has been muted by the argument that what they are seeing and hearing is not oppression at all; it is compliance with laws. But those laws just happen to be rife with ethnocentrism, rejection of the stranger, racism, and structural oppression of the poor.

In this present day of heightened xenophobia, fear, and national isolationism, entire communities are suffering from current and historical trauma. When individual members of designated communities face

---

6. Holmes, *Joy Unspeakable*, 72.

persistent and unthinkable harm or group vulnerability, there is a breaking that occurs which propels that community into a shared experience of crisis contemplation.

> To be flawed, wrong, wounded, is to recognize that we are in a world of other beings. We live and thrive and emerge in the orbit of other beings, and that is beautiful and tragic all at once.[7]

To be human assumes a certain vulnerability. To need the touch that can also wound is an act of faith.

Cyclical Wisdom Patterns

I GREW UP THINKING that disasters were ultimate, that after a crisis, nothing would ever be the same. Of course, I understood that we had to continue with courage, but the grief for "what was" seemed to take up permanent residence in our hearts and minds. I am grateful for the work of Fr. Richard Rohr and his writing about patterns of wisdom. In his book *The Wisdom Pattern,* he describes an organic movement between states of order, disorder, and reorder.[8] Communities are never the same after slavery or the Holocaust or the Trail of Tears, but the shattering of one reality can nurture necessary transformations to meet the issues of another era.

Historical Wounds

THE TERM "HISTORICAL trauma" was coined by Native American social worker and mental health expert Maria Yellow Horse Brave Heart in the 1980s. Brave Heart's definition states that historical trauma "is cumulative emotional and psychological wounding, over the lifespan and across

---

7. Bayo Akomolafe, "Bayo Akomolafe on Reality, Post-Truth and Sacred Activism," *The Future Is Beautiful with Amisha Ghadiali,* podcast, episode 13, May 17, 2018, https://thefutureisbeautiful.libsyn.com/bayo-akomolafe-on-reality-post-truth-and-sacred-activism-e13.

8. Rohr, *The Wisdom Pattern.*

generations, emanating from massive group trauma."[9] Using historical trauma research from studies of survivors of the Holocaust as a starting point,[10] Brave Heart identified six elements of collective trauma in Native generations:

1. First contact: life shock, genocide, no time for grief.
2. Colonialization period: introduction of disease and alcohol, traumatic events such as Wounded Knee Massacre.
3. Invasion/war period: economic competition, sustenance loss (physical/spiritual), extermination, refugee symptoms.
4. Subjugation/reservation period: confined/translocated, forced dependency on oppressor, lack of security.
5. Boarding school period: destroyed family system, beatings, rape, prohibition of Native language and religion. Lasting effect: ill-prepared for parenting, identity confusion.
6. Forced relocation and termination period: transfer to urban areas, prohibition of religious freedom, racism and being viewed as second class; loss of governmental system and community.[11]

Although a detailed discussion of Brave Heart's findings is beyond the scope of this book, I recommend further study of her work and her interviews on YouTube.[12]

---

9. Maria Yellow Horse Brave Heart, "The American Indian Holocaust: Healing Historical Unresolved Grief," *American Indian and Alaska Native Mental Health Research: Journal of the National Center* 8, no. 2 (1998): 56–78, https://pubmed.ncbi.nlm.nih.gov/9842066/. Dr. Maria Yellow Horse Brave Heart is best known for developing a model of historical trauma for the Lakota people, which would eventually be expanded to encompass indigenous populations the world over. She also founded the Takini Network, a non-profit dedicated to the healing of historical trauma in First People.

10. See Laurence J. Kirmayer, Joseph P. Gone, and Joshua Moses, "Rethinking Historical Trauma," *Transcultural Psychiatry* vol. 51, no. 3 (May 22, 2014): 299–319. They contend that there are significant differences between the Native history of trauma and the Holocaust, and include the effects of ongoing structural violence.

11. See also Maria Yellow Horse Brave Heart, "Wakiksuyapi: Carrying the Historical Trauma of the Lakota," *Tulane Studies in Social Welfare* 21–22 (2000): 245–266.

12. For example, "Maria Yellow Horse Brave Heart: Historical Trauma in Native American Populations," *Smith College School for Social Work*, November 4, 2015, https://www.youtube.com/watch?v=RZtCS1362UI.

Dr. Karina Walters agrees with Brave Heart and describes historical trauma as a wounding across generations resulting from a catastrophic event or events experienced over time and across generations by a group of people who share an identity, affiliation, or circumstance.[13] During the past two decades, the term has been applied to Holocaust survivors and numerous colonized indigenous groups throughout the world, as well as to African Americans, Armenian refugees, and Japanese American survivors of internment camps.

Although this listing is not comprehensive, I would also include Palestinian youth, Israelis, Mexicans, and many others who share a history of oppression, victimization, or group trauma exposure. Scholars from various disciplines have described the long-lasting aspects of historical trauma as transgenerational, intergenerational, multi-generational, or cross-generational and have introduced concepts, such as soul wound[14] or Post Traumatic Slavery Syndrome, to capture the collective experience of trauma by specific cultural groups across generations.

We are not surprised that psychic, social, and spiritual effects of trauma reach beyond the actual event of wounding. During collective trauma, individuals experience trauma as part of a group, and that trauma affects their biogenetic descendants. The sobering fact is that we transmit memories, experiences, and our interpretation of those experiences through our genes.

Wounds of Intergenerational Trauma

Natives must learn how their great-grandparents' own pain and suffering can still be impacting them today via epigenetics, in which trauma experienced by earlier generations can influence the

---

13. Karina Walters, "Bodies Don't Just Tell Stories, They Tell Histories: Embodiment of Historical Trauma and Microaggression Distress," *University of Denver Graduate School of Social Work*, March 5, 2012, https://www.youtube.com/watch?v=WzPNWTD56S8.

14. Nathaniel Vincent Mohatt, Azure B. Thompson, Nghi D. Thai, and Jacob Kraemer Tebes, "Historical Trauma as Public Narrative: A Conceptual Review of How History Impacts Present-Day Health," *Social Science & Medicine* 106 (April 2014): 128–136, https://doi.org/10.1016/j.socscimed.2014.01.043.

structure of our genes, making them more likely to "switch on" negative responses to stress and trauma; and via the actual lessons handed down—or not handed down—as a result of institutional trauma such as Indian schools, alcoholism and sexual abuse.[15]

THE MOST DISTRESSING part of collective trauma is its ability to be passed on to subsequent generations. We see the effects of trauma in our children as they struggle with past and present-day injustices. Socioeconomic hardships exacerbate their difficulties. Kenneth Hardy writes, "As with other forms of trauma, we ask the wrong question about struggling youth of color [or culture]. Instead of asking 'What is wrong with them?' we need to ask the trauma-informed question, 'What has happened to them?'"[16]

I might extend that question to include what has happened to intergenerational family members. Since we are addressing wounds, it is important to be specific about the embodied results of racially induced trauma in youth of color/culture. Hardy lifts up the following wounds:

1. **Internalized Devaluation** related to the deification of "whiteness" and the demonization of non-white people.
2. **Assaulted Sense of Self**: During the vulnerable stage of adolescence, youth of color/culture receive unrelenting messages about their lack of intelligence, worth, humanness, and beauty.
3. **Internalized Voicelessness**: The inability to advocate for ourselves or our community. The recognition that, collectively, we are prisoners of the perceptions of others.
4. **The Wound of Rage**: A response to constant devaluation and degradation. Hardy writes, "Youth of color are often prescribed anger management intervention, while rage from the hidden wound of racial oppression remains unaddressed."[17] Young people are more likely to act upon their rage, while elders absorb the poisons into their own bodies, diminishing their health and their wellbeing.

15. Indian Country Today, "Intergenerational Trauma: Understanding Natives' Inherited Pain," *Indian Country Today*, May 10, 2018, https://indiancountrytoday.com/news/intergenerational-trauma-understanding-natives-inherited-pain-HuBOpnz69kSHjN3RsfyRYg#.

16. Hardy, 25.

17. Hardy, 25–26.

Many of these young people are unseen and unheard. Even more distressing is the fact that when they encounter law enforcement, counseling, or attempts to address their needs, the only needs that are addressed are behavioral, without any recognition of the gaping soul wounds left by trauma.

We are learning that the effects of racism also hide at the cellular level. They are embodied and passed down to our descendants through trauma-induced changes in genetic programming.

Epigenetic Effects on Future Generations

> We're just starting to understand that just because you're born with a certain set of genes, you're not in a biologic prison as a result of those genes—that changes can be made to how those genes function, that can help. The idea is a very simple idea, and you hear it from people all the time. People say, when something cataclysmic happens to them, "I'm not the same person. I've been changed. I am not the same person that I was." And epigenetics gives us the language and the science to be able to start unpacking that.[18]

DR. RACHEL YEHUDA, professor of psychiatry at Icahn School of Medicine and Director of the Traumatic Stress Studies Division at Mount Sinai, has conducted research into epigenetics[19] and the intergenerational transmission of trauma. She describes trauma in non-scientific language as "a watershed event, an event that kind of divides your life into a before and after . . . that is cataclysmic, horrible, terrifying—and that changes you."[20]

---

18. Rachel Yehuda, "How Trauma and Resilience Cross Generations," *On Being*, July 30, 2015, updated November 9, 2017, https://onbeing.org/programs/rachel-yehuda-how-trauma-and-resilience-cross-generations-nov2017/.

19. Epigenetics is an emerging field of science that studies heritable changes caused by the activation and deactivation of genes without any change in the underlying DNA sequence of the organism. The word *epigenetics* is of Greek origin and literally means over and above (epi) the genome.

20. As quoted in Kevin Berger, "Ingenious: What PTSD Teaches Us about Both Human Frailty and Resilience," *Nautilus* 31 (December 31, 2015), http://nautil.us/issue/31/stress/ingenious-rachel-yehuda.

Yehuda's research has revealed that when people experience trauma, it changes their genes in a very specific and noticeable way, so when those people have children and their genes are passed down, the children also inherit the genes affected by trauma. Yehuda, who was born in Israel and lived in a predominantly Jewish neighborhood in Cleveland Heights, Ohio, first tested her theory in a small control group of her neighbors who survived the Holocaust.

What she found is that Holocaust survivors had a similar hormonal profile to Vietnam War veterans suffering from PTSD. Our brains have a region called the amygdala, which performs the primary role of processing memory, emotional reactions, and even threat detection. PTSD causes the amygdala to kick into overdrive. It wasn't until years later, after meeting with the child of a Holocaust survivor, that Yehuda decided to determine whether or not traits of trauma were passed down biogenetically. Yehuda's study confirmed her hypothesis.

Post Traumatic Slave Syndrome

AFTER TWELVE YEARS of quantitative and qualitative research, Dr. Joy DeGruy was able to link the trauma of slavery to current generations. Her findings offer a view of historical trauma that aligns with the work of other trauma researchers.[21] She addresses the residual impacts of generations of slavery, institutionalized racism, and the ongoing nature of oppression.

DeGruy's post traumatic slave syndrome (PTSS) theory explains the multiple adaptive survival behaviors in African American communities throughout the United States and the Diaspora. The condition, according to DeGruy, exists as a consequence of the multigenerational oppression of Africans and their descendants, and their creative responses to oppression. DeGruy writes that chattel slavery was predicated on the belief that African Americans were inherently/genetically inferior to whites. The end result for the enslaved was:

---

21. See Joy DeGruy, *Post Traumatic Slave Syndrome: America's Legacy of Enduring Injury and Healing* (Portland, OR: Joy DeGruy Publications, 2017).

M: Multigenerational and collective trauma,

A: absence of opportunities to heal,

P: which leads to PTSS.

Dr. DeGruy describes the trauma of slavery as a condition that altered behaviors and self-regard. Slaves were pitted against one another for work, based on skin color, strength, and ability. Punishment meted out by black overseers further undermined intra-communal trust. As a result of the constant peril, Africans developed both positive and negative adaptive behaviors that allowed them to survive and sometimes even thrive.

But some of the behaviors have been carried over to present times and are maladaptive: mistrust, secret keeping, belittling children to protect them from being sold or forced to work in the fields at a young age. Secret keeping offers a good example. It was useful during slavery but is no longer needed. During slavery, secrets kept or betrayed could be a matter of life and death. Decisions to run away, to pray in the hush arbor, or to start a revolution could not be shared widely or they might be thwarted. Today, communal secret keeping demonstrates a primal distrust that undermines collective purposes and practices.

Trauma comes not only from (1) what has happened to us, but also from (2) what we don't know about our history and (3) our inability to discern our current context. We are now able to trace with accuracy our origins to the continent of Africa through matrilineal and patrilineal genetic tracing. In my family, we have always known my father's probable lineage. His people were "rice growing" Africans from the Senegambia region (probably Sierra Leone). My mother's lineage was a mystery until 2019. Using the services of African Ancestry, we were able to trace her roots to Cameroon and the Tikar people. Of course, Europeans and Asians were included in this line, but not in significant percentages.

For BIPOC communities, there are gaps with regard to our beginnings that many of us learn to fill with guesses about our heritage. When origins cannot be recovered, it is healing to fill in those gaps with stories and art. But when it is possible to follow genetic clues to connect us to continent, nation, and/or tribe, the blessings are quite profound. We are connected to our people, who they were and are.

One of the healthiest options for people who have elected the designation "white" is to explore ethnic and genetic connections to their own indigenous origins. Such explorations might help to dissuade them from the belief that there is a neutral and normal way of being human that is epitomized by "whiteness." If they dig deeply enough into their own genetic history, they will find indigenous communities with practices and lives similar to other indigenous people. The myth of "whiteness" and its superiority was a necessary tool for colonizers that has long outlasted its usefulness.

Body and Soul Wounds

Remember, to the traumatized body, all threats—current or ancient, individual or collective, real or imagined—are exactly the same.[22]

RESMAA MENAKEM REMINDS us that our trauma is located in the body, and that somatic work is crucial to our healing. Harm inflicted on one community affects all, because we are bonded, one to another, at both a scientific and a soul level, whether we like it or not.

We bear not only the residual effects of personal suffering, but the perpetuated crimes against our communities, past and present. The wounds of the elders and ancestors are also ours. We cannot celebrate the fact that we survived when the hatred that inspired the attempted destruction of our communities and our ancestors is still running rampant.

We want to protect our children from the anti-black, anti-BIPOC, anti-LGBTQIA+, anti-women, anti-indigenous sectors of our society. We don't want to be assimilated into a culture that deems us unworthy. The exhausting part of the struggle to be seen as human is that there are so many fronts. Some seem silly, but many are not.

Why should anyone have to prove that they have the right to wear their hair in the way that it grows out of their head?! And yet, there is a news video story that breaks my heart. A young black high school athlete is standing with tears in his eyes. He is being humiliated by a wrestling coach who happens to be white and female. She insists that he allow her

---

22. Menakem, 42–43.

to cut his dreadlocks or forfeit the game.[23] He stands on the court with the audience gasping and takes one for the team as she chops his hair off. He wins the match for his team, picks up his shorn locks, and walks away in spiritual defeat.

But that is not the end of it. Black people are denied graduation, promotions, etc., all because of their hair, black hair. Finally, in the year 2020, it was necessary for Senator Cory Booker to introduce legislation (the Crown Act)[24] to protect African Americans from discrimination as a result of their natural hair. It would seem that folks had more important issues to consider in 2020 than hair. But that's what things come down to: skin color, gender, sexuality, etc., as if these selective elements of our being describe the totality of our humanity.

We are wounded, but not helpless. Some of our wounds are self-inflicted. Others arise because we have disrespected the only habitable planet in our solar system. Our priorities are out of whack, and our values are skewed. We were told that we were to love our neighbors (Mark 12:31), and we set about trying to determine who was in or out of that circle. We were told to depend upon the Divine and, instead, we set about creating abusive economic systems that harm the poor.

> Current research in trauma care . . . has recognized that the stress-reactive dissociation of traumatic experience from prefrontal modulation and left-sided verbal processing makes trauma resistant to conventional psychotherapy.[25]

---

23. NBC News, "NJ High School Wrestler Forced to Cut Dreadlocks," December 21, 2018, https://www.youtube.com/watch?v=ijR-1VZ9vpQ.

24. H.R. 5309, Passed by the 116th Congress, 2019–2020: Creating a Respectful and Open World for Natural Hair Act of 2020 or the Crown Act of 2020. This bill prohibits discrimination based on a person's hair texture or hairstyle if that style or texture is commonly associated with a particular race or national origin. Specifically, the bill prohibits this type of discrimination against those participating in federally assisted programs, housing programs, public accommodations, and employment. Persons shall not be deprived of equal rights under the law and shall not be subjected to prohibited practices based on their hair texture or style. The bill provides for enforcement procedures under the applicable laws.

25. Bessel A. van der Kolk, "The Neurobiology of Childhood Trauma and Abuse," *Child and Adolescent Psychiatric Clinics of North America* 12, no. 2 (April 2003): 293–317, doi: 10.1016/S1056-4993(03)00003-8.

As a result, leading trauma researchers and clinicians are moving toward less discursive, more somatic approaches, including psycho-dramatic re-enactments, narrative and poetic reframing, posture yoga and intensive breath-work.[26]

In these quotes, Dr. Bessel van der Kolk makes it clear that not all of us can talk our way toward healing. Some of us can help our bodies release stored memories and pain by singing and dancing ourselves whole. Perhaps reclaiming our stories and rituals will ease the longing that we have inherited, so that we can invite the Spirit to descend.

We need flaming tongues and reconnections to the specificity of our origins as well as collective responsibility for our villages. We must broaden our identities to include the wisdom of the elders, mystical knowledges forgotten and abandoned. There is so much learning that we can share.

Earth Wounds

The Wounds inflicted on our mother earth are wounds that also bleed in us. . . . We cannot pretend to be healthy in a world that is sick. . . . Caring for ecosystems demands a look to the future, one that is not concerned only with the immediate moment or that seeks a quick and easy profit, but rather one that is concerned for life and that seeks its preservation for the benefit of all.[27]

IN THE QUOTE above, Pope Francis is clear about the connections between our planet and our wellbeing. Although we are all aware that our survival depends upon our planetary mother, we are not always clear

26. Bessel van der Kolk, MD, *The Body Keeps the Score: Mind, Brain and Body in the Transformation of Trauma* (New York: Penguin, 2014), as cited in Joseph J. Loizzo, "Can Embodied Contemplative Practices Accelerate Resilience Training and Trauma Recovery?" *Frontiers in Human Neuroscience*, April 11, 2018, https://www.ncbi.nlm.nih.gov/pmc/articles/PMC5904263/.

27. Pope Francis, as quoted in Mada Jurado, "Pope Laments on World Environment Day: 'The Wounds Inflicted on Our Mother Earth are Wounds that Bleed in Us,'" *Novena*, June 5, 2020, https://novenanews.com/pope-world-environment-day-wounds-mother-earth/.

that her wounds are also ours. His Holiness reminds us that to wound the earth is an act of self-harm.

Indigenous people around the world affirm a similar belief. Luther Standing Bear, writing in the 1930s, noted:

> The old people came literally to love the soil and they sat or reclined on the ground with a feeling of being close to a mothering power. It was good for the skin to touch the earth and the old people liked to remove their moccasins and walk with bare feet on the sacred earth.... The soil was soothing, strengthening, cleansing, and healing.[28]

Our wounds are deep, our wounds are infected, our wounds can be healed.

Summary

THE WOUNDS ARE real. The wounds still seep. How are we to reach out to one another when one or both of us have to stop our efforts at reconciliation to change bandages? It is not the wounding that is ultimate; it is the healing that is always possible. A shift of focus is needed—and if not a shift, then a coexistence of protest and trust that there will be a time when we can put a firm hand on the wound to stop the bleeding, and a time when we will be able to affirm that the trauma occurred but healing is in process.

The wounds that we don't know about or don't remember are the deepest. It is through the wormhole of those wounds that we travel to arrive at the peace that surpasses all understanding. Healing is possible because we have the ability to spiritually veer from disaster, and to allow crises to make rather than break us. Ultimately, we can trust the leading of the Holy Spirit as it guides us toward mutual care and love of God, neighbors, and creation.

---

28. Luther Standing Bear, *Land of the Spotted Eagle* (Lincoln, NE: University of Nebraska Press, 1978), 192; see also Jack D. Forbes, "Indigenous Americans: Spirituality and Ecos," *Dædalus*, Fall 2001, https://www.amacad.org/publication/indigenous-americans-spirituality-and-ecos.

Spiritual Practices

1. Have you or a family or community member ever experienced a collective or historical trauma?
    a. What happened?
    b. If it was resolved, how?
    c. What did the members of the community do while it was happening?
2. Tell the story of a spiritual wound that you, or someone close to you, suffered when you were growing up.
3. Consider this quote by Jim Corbett, goat-walker and co-founder of the Sanctuary Movement:

    "To learn why you feel compelled to remake and consume the world, live alone in wilderness for at least a week. Take no books or other distractions. Take simple, adequate food that requires little or no preparation. Don't plan things to do when the week is over. . . . Simply do nothing."[29]
4. Listen to the YouTube discussion, "Dr. Melanie Harris Making the Connections," Religions for the Earth Conference, Union Theological Seminary, 2014: https://www.youtube.com/watch?v=M7vsZp92yqU. Discuss her view of eco-womanism and environmental justice.

---

29. Jim Corbett, *Goatwalking: A Guide to Wildland Living, a Quest for the Peaceable Kingdom* (New York: Viking, 1991), 5.

After a collective trauma, people tend to sing and move and dance and eat. None of that is incorporated into North American health systems, but most of us who have worked with other cultures, or who have worked with refugees, see how much comfort people get from those activities. Songs and communal sounds that we make let us feel at one with the people around us and are very powerful, very comforting ways of re-establishing connections with other human beings.

—Dr. Bessel van der Kolk

CHAPTER FOUR

THE VILLAGE RESPONSE

It takes a village to raise a child.
—African proverb

I T TAKES A village to survive.

For many of us, villages are a thing of the past. We no longer draw our water from the village well or share the chores of barn raising, sowing, and harvesting. We can get everything—well, almost everything—that we need online. Yet, even though our societies are connected by technology, the rule of law, and a global economy, our relationships are deeply rooted in the memory of local spaces.

Villages are organizational spaces that hold our collective beginnings. They are spaces that we can return to (if only through memory) when we are in need of welcoming and familiar places. What is a village, anyway, but a local group of folks who share experiences, values, and mutual support in common?[1] The functions of such a group may include the fostering and maintenance of common needs, interests, and safety. To put

---

1. David Gurteen, "What Is a Real Community?" *Conversational Leadership,* https://conversational-leadership.net/community/.

it simply, our belonging in these associations includes social and sacred responsibilities to individuals and the group.

Many ethnic communities continue village legacies despite the fact that their "villages" no longer occupy geographical space. Africans have a clear sense of collective belonging that is often preserved in oral wisdom sayings. The adage "It takes a village to raise a child" did not originate with Hillary Clinton's 1996 book title.[2] It only seemed as if she was the source because the idea and the adage were so unfamiliar to dominant culture. BIPOC folks knew firsthand both the saying and the experience of being raised by a village.

I grew up living within the context of village parents (other mothers, male father figures, Aunties, Neighbors, and Big Mamas), who helped to raise me. It really does take a village to raise a child. Generally speaking, most parents don't have all of the tools necessary to meet the needs of their children. The saying addresses village responsibilities to teach the next generation in the ways of the elders and the community.

> Neighborhoods become villages when all of the adults step up to show care and concern for all of the children. . . . In the final analysis, we all live in villages and we all should aspire to transform them into beloved communities.[3]

Although the actual saying may have originated from the Igbo tribe of Nigeria, it is so much a part of African communal culture that it can't be traced definitively to any specific nation or tribe. The Igbo phrase *"Ora Na-azu nwa"* is translated as, "It takes a community or village to raise a child." Lawrence Mbogoni, an African studies professor, wrote:

> Proverb or not, "It takes a whole village to raise a child" reflects a social reality some of us who grew up in rural areas of Africa can easily relate to. As a child, my conduct was a concern of everybody,

---

2. Hillary Rodham Clinton, *It Takes a Village: And Other Lessons Children Teach Us* (New York: Simon & Schuster, 1996). The phrase is ubiquitous throughout African communities, but may have ties to the Igbo people of Nigeria.

3. Robert M. Franklin, *Crisis in the Village: Restoring Hope in African American Communities* (Minneapolis: Fortress, 2007), 3–4.

not just my parents, especially if it involved misconduct. Any adult had the right to rebuke and discipline me and would make my mischief known to my parents who in turn would also mete [out] their own "punishment." The concern of course was the moral well-being of the community.[4]

In the West and in other industrialized nations, nuclear families have severed generational, village, and local connections in favor of privacy and isolation. Because our economic priorities require a mobile workforce, often the market decides where and how we live. When both parents are in the labor force, care for the young and the elderly must be relegated to caregiving businesses. When this occurs, something important is lost.[5]

Without realizing the implications, we have decided that only the knowledges that can be agreed upon, memorized, and transmitted through reading and writing have value. Traditionally, village engagement in the raising of children included introduction into the mysteries of the elders and ancestral realm.

Malidoma Somé writes, "While a grandfather is alive, the grand-children do not have much of anything to learn from their father—until they reach their preadolescent age. And the father knows that."[6] The child has recently come from the realm of the ancestors and the grandparents are on their way. There is much wisdom and special knowledge to be imparted between these generations. So, the parents encourage the development of strong relationships between children and elders. Villages of care and training in African communal cultures include elders, neighbors, an introduction to everyday mysticism, and the spiritual vibrancy of multiple realities.

---

4. As quoted in Joel Goldberg, "It Takes a Village to Determine the Origins of an African Proverb," *NPR*, July 30, 2016, https://www.npr.org/sections/goatsand-soda/2016/07/30/487925796/it-takes-a-village-to-determine-the-origins-of-an-afri-can-proverb. See also Madelaine Hron, "'Ora Na-Azu Nwa': The Figure of the Child in Third-Generation Nigerian Novels," *Research in African Literatures* 39:2 (Summer 2008), 27–48.

5. Discussions with Ched Myers, biblical scholar and the author of *The Biblical Vision of Sabbath Economics* (Washington, DC: Tell the Word Press, 2001).

6. Malidoma Patrice Somé, *Of Water and the Spirit: Ritual, Magic and Initiation in the Life of an African Shaman* (New York: Penguin, 1994), 21.

In this book, I am using the word "village" to invoke similar spiritual and tribal commitments and obligations. The word "village" also makes reference to the tangle of relationships that are included in these social collectives. Sometimes villages are structured and complex, sometimes fleeting and ephemeral. But always there is a shared sense of identity, responsibility, belonging, and spiritual expansiveness. When there is a crisis, it takes a village to survive.

The Power of Belonging

> A sense of belonging is what keeps people in communities. This belonging is the goal of community building. The hallmark of a strong community is when its members feel that they belong.
>
> —Jono Bacon, *The Art of Community:*
> *Building the New Age of Participation*

DURING TIMES OF peace and "normalcy," belonging is the glue that holds communities together. During times of crisis, belonging to one community or another may heighten a threat, but may also increase the potential for survival of the group. During the period of crisis, there is more potential for survival if the village can revive the bonds of culture, ritual, and voice.

An example comes to mind. Africans bought and stolen from Africa's shores were targeted as laborers who could help to build the new world. But, it is also a fact that some Africans were enslaved in Africa by Africans. The difference between the chattel slavery of the West and the practice of slavery in Africa was that those enslaved in Africa as a result of inter-tribal conflict or an indentured servant arrangement were allowed to keep their culture and religious practices, and were incorporated into the community. They belonged.

In the Americas, the humanity of Africans was violated, their cultural practices and rituals were forbidden, and their separation from society was mandated by law. They were treated, then and now, as if they did not belong. Despite these impediments, African diasporan and indigenous communities survived through the creative blending of tribal customs, the development of inter-communal bonds, and the creation of new practices.

> We are collective creatures. We don't exist as individuals. Our brain is meant to be in synchrony with other brains. Interaction with other brains fundamentally shapes who we are. When we cry, we're supposed to get a response, and when we laugh, somebody is supposed to laugh with us.[7]

We survive as a people because we collectively nurture one another. We respond to need and trauma as a village. This village does not require proximity or sameness to respond. It is based on a sense of shared experiences. Belonging matters. Our lives together matter.

Who Is My Neighbor?

MOST JUDEO-CHRISTIAN FAITH traditions tell us to "love our neighbors as ourselves." Buddhists, Muslims, and others include this requirement as a central tenet in their belief system. Examples from varied faith traditions seem to reflect the universality of this concept.

Confucianism

What you do not want done to yourself, do not do to others. (Analects 15–23)

Judeo-Christian

You shall not take vengeance or bear a grudge against any of your people, but you shall love your neighbor as yourself: I am the Lord. (Leviticus 19:18)

In everything do to others as you would have them do to you; for this is the law and the prophets. (Matthew 7:12)

---

7. Bessel van der Kolk, as quoted in Elissa Melaragno, "Trauma in the Body: An Interview with Dr. Bessel van der Kolk," *Daily Good: News that Inspires*, April 21, 2018, http://www.dailygood.org/story/1901/trauma-in-the-body-an-interview-with-dr-bessel-van-der-kolk/.

This is my commandment, that you love one another as I have loved you. (John 15:12)

Islam

Serve Allah, and join not any partners with Him; and do good—to parents, kinsfolk, orphans, those in need, neighbors who are near, neighbors who are strangers, the companion by your side, the wayfarer (you meet), and what your right hands possess: For Allah loveth not the arrogant, the vainglorious. (Qur'an 4:36)

Buddhism

A state that is not pleasing or delightful to me, how could I inflict that upon another? (Samyutta Nikaya v. 353)

Despite the clarity of the sacred texts, not many of us live out these simple guidelines for happiness and peace. We seem stuck, quibbling over how we define the word "neighbor." Are neighbors the people who live next door and play their music too loud? Are neighbors the immigrants who are moving into the village in larger and larger numbers?

For too long, Western nations have defined neighbors as people who fit into their surroundings or have the same skin color, language, and ethnicity. The definition is further complicated by biblical and dictionary definitions that limit neighbors to those who live in proximity with us. But what does proximity mean when the internet connects us across vast geographical stretches and when we belong to many "villages," some based on politics, others based on social designations, ethnicity, gender/sexuality, or faith?

It's a fallacy of our modern lives to assume that the concept of a "neighborhood" only encompasses a select group of people: our actual neighbors, our coworkers, our family, our partners. In truth, our neighborhoods are vastly more sprawling and interconnected than we frequently choose to acknowledge. My neighborhood is a vast network of taxi drivers, the guy who delivers my pizza, the cashiers at the mall, the baristas at my favorite coffee shops, the woman at the dry cleaners, the bartenders at my local dive, the voice on the other end of the customer service hotline, the custodians at the theaters where I work.[8]

In the quote above, Katherine Fritz recognizes that neighbors are defined by relationships, brief or recurring, that emerge and recede during daily life. Some neighbors abide and then move on, others share deeply resonant relations, yet others connect to us in brief but recurring episodes. When all the pieces of the life puzzle are moving, static definitions will not do.

In each generation, we are tested. Will we love our neighbors as ourselves or will we measure our responsibilities to one another in accordance with whomever we deem to be "in" or "out" of our social circles? And what of those unexpected moments of crisis, those critical events that place an entire village at risk? How do we survive together? How do we resist together? How do we respond to unspeakable brutality and the collective oppression of our neighbors?

Our lifelong efforts to map our uniqueness do not defeat our collective connections. Although I am an individual with a name, family history, and embodiment as an African American woman, I am also inextricably connected to several "villages" that reflect my social, cultural, national, spiritual, and generational identifications. These connections require that I respond and resist when any village is under assault.

Community Constellations

I AM RETIRED NOW, but when I was younger, I always knew that I was not alone. There was a community with me in my present reality; there was an ancestral community in another reality, holding me safe; and there were communities unfamiliar to me whose historical trajectory paralleled mine and could teach me something.

The Now Community

The community members who lived in the neighborhood and waved hello helped me to envision a future. They went to church, told

8. Katherine Fritz, "These Are the People in Your Neighborhood," *HuffPost*, November 24, 2014, https://www.huffpost.com/entry/these-are-the-people-in-y_b_6204468?.

the stories of resilience and folk medicine, gossiped, and made me laugh. They believed in God, respected their preachers, but did not believe that because your collar was turned backward, you were immune from everyday human failings.

They helped me to understand village life on macro and micro levels. I grew up with a healthy wariness of dominant culture, yet the elders did not warn us as I warned my sons. The elders told stories about their encounters and did not interpret. I am clear as to where the dangers lie with current policing, and I give my sons specific ways to de-escalate any encounter with law enforcement.

As I reflect, I'm not sure that my way has been better. The elders viewed police violence from the lens of fallen humanity and quoted scripture as they shared. I burdened my children with my own fears and resentments of police brutality. I wanted my children and others like them to survive the police encounter. In retrospect, I should have included with my warnings the fact that the fear of difference is a shared human trait, and that the fact of our interconnectivity will not allow us to separate, based on skin color or political views. This is a bigger theological and philosophical issue than I imagined. Talks with now-grown sons reflect the need to keep all of us safe, to protest when necessary, to negotiate when possible, and to work out resolutions to institutionalized racism with contemplative hearts and centered passions.

The Community of the Ancestors/Elders

A world without ancestors is lonely. I am so grateful for the elders in my family who introduced me to the continuums in life. It matters how we understand our sojourn in this reality. If we consider our lives to be comprised of segments separated by a dash that encompasses birth and death dates, we will be inconsolable when trauma truncates our realities and delays our destinations. But, if we consider ourselves to be part of a continuum of life that does not end with death, but transitions to a life after life, our perspectives can change.

The community of the ancestors, already inhabiting the life beyond life, kept in constant contact with us. They sent messages and intervened when necessary. They prayed with me and whispered warnings. But, not every person who dies is an ancestor. The definition includes certain assumptions. Whether we call them ancestors or elders, only those women and men who led good lives in the physical realm are considered to be wise guides in the spiritual realm. In some African cultures, they are called elders, "the old ones." Any elder represents the entire legal and mystical authority of the lineage. For me, ancestors, living and dead elders, commanded my respect and were always present, abiding and guiding me.

Here is the perplexing truth! I did not pass on these lifegiving realities to my children. I adopted Western and dominant cultural values that propelled me toward tangible accomplishments and education. I wanted to model for my sons what the dream articulated by King would look like—and by doing so, missed opportunities to connect my sons to their deeply rooted spiritual ancestry.

Neighbors under Siege

WHEN WE COME together to protest white supremacy, a question inevitably arises from dominant cultures: "If you are so concerned about your community, why do blacks kill blacks with regularity?" It is a question intended to deflect focus from the systematized slaughter of brown/black bodies by the institutions that enforce white supremacy. I cannot provide an answer for each and every instance of intra-communal violence. I do know that among every group there are those whose behavior is outside of professed norms.

> White people kill thousands of white people every year and no one ever talks about "white-on-white crime." Googling "white-on-white crime" returns 2,200,000 results in .034 seconds; Googling black-on-black crime on the other hand returns 1,110,000,000 results in 0.45 seconds. That is 50 times more results for the term black-on-black crime. It has become a part of the English language in a way that white-on-white crime has not.[9]

9. Reggie Jackson, "Stop Accusing the Black Lives Matter Movement of Ignoring So-Called 'Black-on-Black' Crime," *Milwaukee Independent*, July 13, 2020, http://www.milwaukeeindependent.com/featured/stop-accusing-black-lives-matter-movement-ignoring-called-black-black-crime/.

The disparate numbers do not indicate that there are more black-on-black crimes. It indicates that crimes in the white community against one another are not categorized by race. Beyond this obvious response, I would add that oppression has consequences. What we don't seem to recognize is that violence is not a racial characteristic or tendency. Often, it is an unhealthy response to poverty and oppression. What seems to dominant culture like the inherent lawlessness of some BIPOC communities is a consequence of social and economic marginalization, and a lack of emotional and spiritual connections to a village. What's needed is an antidote to the racism that destroys the nonviolent and violent alike. Although there are no easy solutions, perhaps the re-establishment of village connections can offer a starting point.

Is History Repeating Itself?

IT IS IMPOSSIBLE to talk about a village response to crisis without glancing backward at the history of the human rights violations of our nation. Our open racial animosities and fear of the stranger indicate that we have not learned our lessons from history.

Internationally, the situation is similar. England's Brexit vote included anti-immigrant sentiments that have been simmering for years:

> Reports of xenophobia and racism have piled up in the media: the fire-bombing of a halal butchers in Walsall, graffiti on a Polish community center in London and laminated cards reading: "No more Polish vermin" apparently posted through letterboxes in Huntingdon. . . . [Sociologist Paul Baguley] says, "This has been the bedrock and basis for this xenophobia, directed at everybody who is a little different. It is unlike the backlash after terrorist attacks, which targeted Irish people in the 70s, or Muslims and those thought to be Muslims, more recently. It is a very generalized kind of racism oriented against any groups perceived not to be in that narrow category of white English identity."[10]

10. Homa Khaleeli, "'A Frenzy of Hatred': How to Understand Brexit Racism," *The Guardian*, June 29, 2016, https://www.theguardian.com/politics/2016/jun/29/frenzy-hatred-brexit-racism-abuse-referendum-celebratory-lasting-damage.

Both Britain and the US are conflicted. As both nations pursue isolationist political policies, their citizens of every ethnic origin are participating in protests to affirm that Black Lives Matter. Meanwhile, the US is still holding migrant adults and children in deplorable conditions at the US-Mexico border. Several children have died, food is inadequate, and the crisis is escalating as more and more unaccompanied children seek entry.

Both Britain and the US also seem to be yearning for a less diverse future, a return to a familiar order that prioritized the needs of "white people." But the definition of "whiteness" is cultural and fluid. Take a look at the definition of "white" in the 2020 US census:

> The category "White" includes all individuals who identify with one or more nationalities or ethnic groups originating in Europe, the Middle East, or North Africa. Examples of these groups include, but are not limited to, German, Irish, English, Italian, Lebanese, Egyptian, Polish, French, Iranian, Slavic, Cajun, and Chaldean.[11]

This definition has nothing to do with "science." As the Census Bureau carefully notes, "The U.S. Census Bureau must adhere to the 1997 Office of Management and Budget (OMB) standards on race and ethnicity which guide the Census Bureau in classifying written responses to the race question." The census goes on to note that the racial categories on the questionnaire "reflect a social definition of race recognized in this country and not an attempt to define race biologically, anthropologically, or genetically."[12]

So, we are dealing with a social construct that has no basis in fact, and yet the impact is powerful. To be identified as "white" has real consequences in the Americas. Although the census form states that the citizen filling out the census can select their identities (they can choose more than one category), the "white" category counterintuitively includes Middle Easterners and North Africans.

---

11. "2020 Census Questions: Race," *United States Census 2020*, https://2020census. gov/en/about-questions/2020-census-questions-race.html.

12. "About Race," *United States Census Bureau*, https://www.census.gov/topics/ population/race/about.html.

We have the ability to struggle with and confront race and deconstruct it where it legally exists. We need to stop separating people. If we root out and destroy any benefit created by race classification, it is only then that we will overcome it.[13]

On a spiritual level, it seems that we are howling into the wind. The sciences tell us that we are connected no matter how separated we may seem. Yet, we choose to continue a fiction that benefits some, but not all, of us. Lord have mercy.

Thank You for Pain

I bring You my pain
I bring You my sorrow
I bring You my shame
The threat of tomorrow
I've heard that You're close to the
Broken-hearted and near to the cries of the poor
Well prove it, I'm on the floor
I'll wait[14]

The poet says what we want to say: "Where are You? We have read of your power and penchant for justice, so . . . ??? Do You see us? I am not here alone; a whole village is at risk. Don't worry, we'll wait."

As I get older and live through the many crises that affect human communities, I am becoming more and more aware that lament may be an important first option and response to crisis for individuals and for entire villages. Ellen Davis puts it this way:

If in this place tears are not just tolerated but required of us from time to time, it is because the thirst for God that brought each of us

13. Francys Johnson, "Race Is Fiction. Racism Is Not," *The Sanders Institute*, March 2014, https://www.sandersinstitute.org/blog/race-is-fiction-racism-is-not.

14. Aaron Niequist, "Thank You for Pain," in *No. 7: Lament*, 2019, *A New Liturgy*, https://www.anewliturgy.com/no-7-lament. Used with permission.

to this place has at the same time drawn us into the very center of a sustained conflict.[15]

Our tears can be refreshment, a type of baptism, a salty preservation, a sign of vulnerability, and a liturgical response to violence. Lament is weird, but it works—and it may not work in the way that we expect. We think that if we can just get the sorrow out and excavate the deep furrows of pain, that we will be alright. But the truth of the matter is that we have to be alright with the pain, with the furrows, and with the lack of answers as to why bad things happen to good people. We also have to recover the art of lament.

Lament

Communal lament is important for several reasons. It wakes us up and, in doing so, makes us mindful of the pain of our neighbors, who no longer can go about business as usual when the women begin to wail. Their keening rattles both marrow and bone. Who can remain in a stupor with all of that yelling?! But lament is important for another reason: The collective wail reminds us that we are not alone. The sheer power and resonance of a grief-stricken chorus reminds us that we are beings of quantum potential. We still have agency in every cell of our being, enough to survive—even this!

Lament is risky business, or, as Walter F. Brueggemann would say, "risky speech." The reasons that lament is risky are because it challenges power structures, it calls for justice, and it makes demands on our relationships with the "powers that be," one another, and God. Once lament is released, it cannot be recalled. Lament is risky because we never know until the act is done whether or not we have gone too far.[16]

Lament allows the pain to escape and stitches us to our neighbors. We are called to weep with those who weep and mourn with those who mourn. Our tears are our prayers when we can't speak, a baptism of

---

15. Ellen Davis, "I Thirst," *In Trust*, Autumn 2005, https://www.intrust.org/Magazine/Issues/Autumn-2005/I-thirst.

16. I studied under Walter Brueggemann in seminary. For more on this topic, see Walter F. Brueggemann, *The Psalms and the Life of Faith*, ed. Patrick D. Miller (Minneapolis: Augsburg Fortress, 1995).

sorts, a salty healing, a sign of our vulnerability, and a liturgical response to violence.

Lament gives us back our voices. We are a silenced people. Our technology hypnotizes us. The pundits speak for us on such a regular basis that silence seems normal. We don't know what to say and so we say nothing. Lament says something, even if the something is just a gasp or a moan.

Lament is a collective response to tyranny and injustice. When we are confronted with the horror of our violence-laden society, our mindless killing of innocents, we shift from individual sob and solitary whine to collective moans. I introduced the research of James Noel and my own Middle Passage studies about the moan in the chapter on Wounds. Here, I reference the moan as a village response to trauma. We moan to hear one another and for assurance that we are not alone.

In similar fashion, the Holy Spirit groans prayers on our behalf. In the Epistle to the Romans (8:26, NIV) Paul states, "In the same way, the Spirit helps us in our weakness. We do not know what we ought to pray for, but the Spirit . . . intercedes for us through wordless groans."

Throughout Romans chapter 8, Paul writes of sacred utterances of creation and humankind in crisis. We don't know what will emerge from this time of tarrying, but we do know that something is being born. Like a woman in labor, there is expectation in the darkness, anticipation amid the suffering, hope permeating the pain. Something new is being born and something old is being transformed. The village moan prepares us for public lament.

It is lament that prepares us for action and resistance. It is art that heals our weary souls.

Art as a Response to Trauma

WHILE IT IS true that protest is as American as apple pie, it is not helpful to use this example of alignment with national values when BIPOC people are under siege. Yes, revolt is threaded throughout the founding of America, but we must be careful with analogies. BIPOC are not afforded the same rights as dominant culture, as evidenced by the insurrection on

January 6, 2021, when white Trump supporters were allowed to breach the Capitol Building. By comparison, black and brown bodies protesting police murders are treated as if they are a threat to the entire social order.

Once this determination is made, revolution is no longer a safe option for social change, unless it is spiritual. The Civil Rights movement is a recent example. The leaders did not argue that they were resisting in accordance with American revolutionary ideals. Instead, they argued that nonviolent Christian principles undergirded the movement. A purportedly Christian nation could not argue against that premise. But when there is a movement, a demonstration of the commitment of bodies and lives, there must also be an attempt to change hearts. This job is assigned to the arts.

> How does art heal? Scientific studies tell us that art heals by changing a person's physiology and attitude. The body's physiology changes from one of stress to one of deep relaxation, from one of fear to one of creativity and inspiration.[17]

Creating art together is a healing response that the village can use to begin to bind up wounds. Artistic expression invites spiritual presence and conjures the much-needed mending of body and soul. Having worked for several years as an actor in professional companies, I can state that rehearsal and mastery of the craft opens pathways for s(S)pirit to have its way with the story that is being told. For the first few performances, actors are telling the story to an audience. Soon thereafter, the story takes on a life of its own. Through whispers of the playwright's intent, and the reaction of the audience, the characters inhabit the story and guide the actors' choices. It is a haunting experience.

> Art and music put a person in a different brain wave pattern; art and music affect a person's autonomic nervous system, their hormonal balance and their brain neurotransmitters.

---

17. Monte Nagler, "How Art Heals: Mind-Body Physiology," *Photos for Healing Newsletter* 122 (January 2018), https://www.montenagler.com/wp-content/uploads/2018/01/Photos-for-Healing-Newsletter-122-Jan.-18.pdf.

Art and music affect every cell in the body instantly to create a healing physiology that changes the immune system and blood flow to all the organs. Art and music also immediately change a person's perceptions of their world. They change attitude, emotional state, and pain perception. They create hope and positivity and they help people cope with difficulties. They transform a person's outlook and way of being in the world.[18]

For me, the difference that art makes for the village is that it provides a language fit for the task of spiritual engagement with the "powers that be."[19] The old languages and protests have grown stale.

We need new paths. . . . I say . . . unleash the primal on the familiar, disturb the edges, dispute the layers, find a place of stillness, press your ears to the ground to feel the rumblings of things outside your philosophy, linger by the shrubbery, improvise new rituals, pay homage to the nonhuman, and acknowledge the wilds whence you came.[20]

We need languages that are transformative and mystical, languages poetic, theatrical, and musical that evoke our commonalities. We are relying still on tried-and-true protests and public action that no longer have the power to help us to imagine more.

The best response of the village to police violence is the same as it was during the Civil Rights movement: creative expression and art. We speak poetry and rap rhythms of survival. We offer graffiti images of the slain. We dance and let our bodies reveal our suffering and persistence. And, when all else fails, we sing ourselves sane. Art opens a portal to new realities.

---

18. Nagler.

19. See Walter Wink's books *Naming the Powers, Unmasking the Powers,* and *Engaging the Powers.*

20. Bayo Akomolafe, "Release the Kraken: Why We Need Monsters in These Times of Crises," initially published in *Revolutionary Wellness Magazine,* May 20, 2020, https://bayoakomolafe.net/project/release-the-kraken-why-we-need-monsters-in-these-times-of-crises/.

At the deepest level, creativity is holiness.
—John O'Donohue

Locating Grief Together

Trauma is not the story of something that happened back then.... It's
the current imprint of that pain, horror, and fear living inside people.
—Bessel A. van der Kolk

WE HOLD OUR grief in our bodies. When we experience collective
trauma, the grief seems to be dispersed because it is so difficult to locate.
Grief invades and silently spreads, setting up its own altars in our bodies.
It does not go away any more than the loss of a loved one does. Embodied
grief throbs and then lessens until we can no longer locate its habitations,
but the body knows. Communal rituals, dance and song, storytelling and
sacred remembrance illuminate the grief-stricken inner spaces so that we
can heal.

Summary

THE WAY INTO a future that is not yet on the horizon is through the performance of imagination and hope, watercolor and oil, choral attestations
of faith and resistance to the status quo. The village is together and in one
accord. We will not continue to play professional sports while you kill our
friends and neighbors. We will not participate in endless conversations
about systemic racism.

We will not pick your crops while you cage our children. We will not
accept your truncated view of reality or your disbelief in the connectedness of life. We cannot predict the future, but we can take a transcendent
leap toward the unknown. We will strengthen one another and heal ourselves, our communities, and our world/planet. Ashe!

Lament + Art + Locating Grief Together

Practices of Lament

1. The village knows that it is under siege, that it would be better to leave the Americas, and yet we stay. Harriet Tubman had to walk, but we can fly away, and still we stay. We remember the beginnings of the Holocaust, the fear and the warnings, and yet most German Jewish communities did not flee. Perhaps we are facing another Katrina moment: There is nowhere to go, no money to relocate, no vehicles to transport folks. Or perhaps we have deluded ourselves into believing that history will not repeat itself. Why do we stay? **Sit with this reality. What comes up for you?**

2. After another police murder attempt, the village responds, and once again grief is being expressed through protests. White supremacist groups race to the location to heighten the unrest. The National Guard has been called in, and, once again, the tables have been turned. Now, the people who are protesting are being gunned down as enemies of the city and of the social order. White community leaders must save their downtown businesses, and so this marauding mob must be stopped with curfews and more violence. **Sit with this reality. What comes up for you?**

3. Read the story of Rizpah (2 Samuel 21:1–14). Rizpah cannot stop David from killing her sons, so she does not beg or bargain. Instead, what were her practices?

   a. She bears silent witness, identifies her strengths, and protects what's left. What are your strengths? Name three.

   b. Rizpah appears to be alone, but she also knows that an entire society, her village of belonging, is watching.

   c. Because David will not allow the dead to be buried, Rizpah fights birds and beasts for six months or more as she guards the bodies of her sons. In so doing, she shames David and he, in turn, allows them to be buried.

4. Identify the slain innocents today. What can be done? What can you do?

   a. Which of Rizpah's practices make sense for our lives, and which don't?

   b. Name practices, laws, etc., in your community or nation that harm people and take away their power.

   c. What would Rizpah do? What will you do?

5. Write a lament regarding an issue of deep concern. Use the following elements.

   a. Protest: Tell God what is wrong.

   b. Petition: Tell God what you want God to do about it.

   c. Praise: Write expressions of trust and praise, based on God's character and action in the past, even if you can't see the outcome of your petition.

Art Practices

Art washes away from the soul the dust of everyday life.
—Pablo Picasso

1. Prepare art supplies of your choosing for intuitive or soul art. Choose a medium that is not part of your ordinary spiritual practice. If you are a poet, paint. If you are a painter, take photos. This creative spiritual practice does not focus on the outcome or result of the activity. This is a practice that allows what is in you to come into focus. Explore and open yourself to new avenues of creativity.

2. *Coelo Divina*: art as a spiritual practice. *Lectio Divina* is an ancient practice of meditation from the Christian tradition in which you delve more deeply into a text, allowing it to speak to you in surprising and hopeful ways. *Coelo Divina* takes this practice and adds a responsive time of art journaling, using pens, paint, graphite. Let your art speak to you and surprise you.[21]

---

21. For further inspiration, watch Lou Davis, "Coelo Divina: Art as a Spiritual Practice," *YouTube*, October 3, 2016, https://www.youtube.com/watch?v=VKiEpVfrJ7w.

3. Look for and photograph "God" in nature.
4. Create an art journal using a word or theme that has meaning for you.[22]

Locating Grief Practices

1. Drumming circles are a village response to the mystery of being and brokenness. With every beat, we evoke the wisdom of the elders and the embrace of the divine.
2. As a group, use a movement exercise that heightens your resonance. Move or dance together for at least 15 minutes, then sit and breathe, silently asking your body where the trauma is hiding. What do you need from the village to heal the wounds?
3. Locate the communal grief in your body. Mark it on the image on the next page if you like. Sit with it in silence.[23]
4. Locate the grief in your village. Share your insights.
5. Close by singing a comforting communal song.

---

22. For further inspiration, watch Bare Branch Blooming, "Themed Gluebook – Art as a Spiritual Practice," *YouTube*, October 20, 2019, https://www.youtube.com/watch?v=pbozHbTz6Ug.

23. This exercise is inspired by Bessel van der Kolk's *The Body Keeps the Score: Brain, Mind, and Body in the Healing of Trauma* (New York: Penguin, 2014) and Natalie Goldberg's *Writing Down the Bones: Freeing the Writer Within* (Boston: Shambhala, 1986).

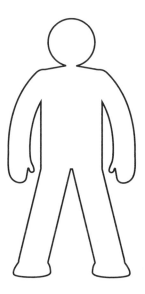

Your Body

Your Village

It feels like everything is broken. We must, each of us, fix our attention on the nearest wound, conjure within us the smallest parts of ourselves that are still whole, and be healers. Heal with words and prayer and energy, heal with money, clean water, time and action. . . . Our visions are ropes through the devastation. Look further ahead, like our ancestors did, look further.

Extend, hold on, pull,

evolve.

—Adrienne Maree Brown

CHAPTER FIVE

HEALING

May our individual tears moisten the soil of our common humanity, germinating seeds of hope, compassion and mercy that will blossom and heal our collective suffering.

—Dedan Gills and Belvie Rooks,
I Give You the Springtime of My Blushing Heart: A Poetic Love Song

I AM A GARDENER, a lover of dark soil and rooted mysteries. The fact that flowers, herbs, and vegetables eventually burst forth from dampened seeds is always a wonder. It is also a joyful surprise when people who have been harmed to the extreme find peace and healing, even while trauma continues.

My anecdotal observations of my own community have convinced me that the roots of healing are deeply sown by the same s(S)pirit that hovered over creation during the "Let there be" transformation of the world. The shamans and root workers, aunties and folk healers long gone taught us that everything we needed to heal us was within our reach. Even salty tears could cure raw wounds if we could stand the pain.

What Would Healing Look Like?

DEDAN GILLS (1945–2015) and Belvie Rooks, co-founders of Growing a Global Heart, tell the story of their visit to the slave departure point in Ghana and the wrenching pain that ensued. Belvie was in Ghana to marry Dedan, and yet the sorrow of historical trauma was overwhelming the celebratory occasion. The full story of their encounter with the wounds of slavery on the continent of Africa can be found in their book, *I Give You the Springtime of My Blushing Heart.*

In this discussion, I want to focus on Dedan's question to Belvie: What would healing look like? His question reverberates throughout time and applies to communal as well as individual trauma. What does healing look like for communities overwhelmed by ongoing trauma? How does community survive? Those of us who were raised in communities under siege can tell you that there are many coping mechanisms.

As one of the first steps toward healing and survival, we take a big gulp of reality. We have to admit that we have been broken before we can be healed. We can't heal until we can grieve the events that have wounded us, release the spiritual toxins left behind, and open ourselves to something new. Communal grieving offers something that we cannot get when we grieve by ourselves. In the words of Sobonfu Somé, "Through validation, acknowledgement and witnessing, communal grieving allows us to experience a level of healing that is deeply and profoundly freeing."[1] During the worst of times, we must collectively listen for the rustle of the s(S)pirit and ready ourselves to "move when the Spirit says move."[2]

It's Not Personal

There is a point on our healing journey where we realize it is no longer personal. Our pain, the pain of our ancestry, is the pain of the world, and vice versa. Our healing is for humanity. We perceive the

---

1. Sobonfu Somé, "Embracing Grief: Surrendering to Your Sorrow Has the Power to Heal the Deepest of Wounds," originally published in *Alternatives* 40 (Winter 2006), http://www.sobonfu.com/articles/writings-by-sobonfu-2/embracing-grief/.
2. Traditional Gospel hymn.

pain of the world clearer than ever, and feel it through our broken-heartedness. It can no longer be denied, and therefore we can no longer pretend that the pain of women in Saudi Arabia or the pain of children in Syria is not our own. It is collective pain and we are part of that collective, the one body of humanity we are part of. Healing then takes on a whole new purpose.[3]

IN A PERFECT world, I would describe this purpose as a shedding of false identities and desires, a scraping away of layers of untruth, a revelation of connections that are inescapable and transforming. Healing after collective trauma gives us an opportunity to *view the world differently*, to open ourselves to new teachings from unexpected teachers. Bayo Akomolafe puts it this way:

> I learned that plants communicate with each other, and respond to emotions; that brittle-stars manage to do well without using brains; that bees have society and complex social rituals for navigating their environment; that orcas have been known to perform their own experiments on the human researchers that study them; that light is either a particle or a wave depending on the apparatus used to measure "it"—which is to say that the world has no pre-relational, determinate quality except within the context of relationships; that time isn't linear and that originary points are not necessary to explain the world; and, that we live and thrive and die in the entangling orbit of other beings.[4]

We instinctively know what Akomolafe is talking about as soon as we enter this plane of existence. But what does healing mean when the trauma never ends, when each generation must confront the same monsters? If

---

3. Vince Gowmon, "Awakening to Darkness—Feeling Below the Threshold of Pseudo Spirituality and Light Chasing," *Vince Gowmon: Healing for a New World*, www.vincegowmon.com/awakening-to-darkness.

4. As quoted in "Bayo Akomolafe: The Meaning of Life . . . in Its Stunning Material Vibrancy," *Excellence Reporter*, March 6, 2018, https://excellencereporter.com/2018/03/06/bayo-akomolafe-the-meaning-of-life-in-its-stunning-material-vibrancy/.

we are to survive as communities of color/culture, we must heal while we are on the go! That means we must protest and resist violence and oppression, while developing/reclaiming creative options that will restore the village. We must shed our indoctrinations to a way of life that is unnatural, feed our spirits, and seek opportunities to share our gifts.

My hope rests upon the multiplicity of gifts that are intrinsic to village life. Some will pray, others will resist, still others will teach the generations on the rise and yet others will go inward toward discernment of the Spirit. I know that it is difficult to continue our spiritual practices while our communities are being terrorized by random violence, and so I offer three specific ways to move toward healing: through the recovery of memory and story, the revival of culture and ritual, and the interpretation of our trauma through the lens of our joy.

We are part of something bigger than an individual existence. Purpose and entanglement, collectivity and potential are part of the tapestry of life. The temptation is to accumulate and compete, activities that do not enhance the community or the soul. The collective task is to de-center our human hubris, delight in the enchantment of a shared and inspirited life space, and tell our stories.

Telling Our Stories

Stories worth their salt don't tell us to get cranked up with either naïve hope or vinegar-tinged despair. Stories tell us to keep attending to the grace. Keep an eye on the miraculous.[5]

WE ARE REVIVED by the stories that we tell about our reality, our bodies, our spirits, and our God. These stories challenge and unsettle us. They touch us in places that facts seldom reach and often move us to action. Most religions have more stories than anything else. Whenever Jesus is asked a question, he answers with a story, a parable. "He did not say anything to them without using a parable" (Matthew 13:34, NIV).

---

5. Martin Shaw, "The Radical Power of Storytelling," *Yes Magazine*, March 10, 2020, https://www.yesmagazine.org/health-happiness/2020/03/10/radical-power-story-telling.

We tell our stories because all of us have survived something, because stories are signposts from the past that give us clues about the future. Finally, our stories are a witness to the next generation and an opportunity to understand the universal as well as the particular in tales of trauma, healing, and survival.

The business of stories is not enchantment.
The business of stories is not escape.
The business of stories is waking up.[6]

When I allow myself to succumb to storytelling, I sense connections to others that I seldom notice. I hear the black community's story in the stories of Jewish persecution and the attempts to destroy the cultures of Native people in the Americas. My memories are specific to the sacred stories of my village, but these stories also resonate with others who have endured similar circumstances.

Recovery of Memory and Story

WE NOW KNOW that historical trauma can be passed down genetically to future generations. How do we heal when the trauma is accompanied by the silence of the elders and their (understandable) reluctance to share the stories of grief and loss? Trauma therapists agree that communal and individual healing are aided by the recovery of history, the documentation of atrocities, the naming of the nameless, and the restoration of our "collective identities and stories."[7] Debra Hosseini describes one of the elements of PTSD as

an inability to construct a coherent story of our past. Traumatic memory is like a series of still snapshots without music or words that reside in the right hemisphere of our brains. The left side of the brain

---

6. Shaw.

7. Taasogle Daryl Rowe and Kamilah Marie Woodson, "How to Heal African-Americans' Traumatic History," *The Conversation*, June 19, 2018, https://theconversation.com/how-to-heal-african-americans-traumatic-history-98298.

does the thinking. Emotional and cognitive disassociation between the two sides of the brain occurs during traumatic events. The part of the brain that is most impacted by traumatic events is the Broca, the center for speech. The amygdala, the hypothalamus, and the prefrontal cortex are also affected by traumatic events.[8]

Many of the clinical specialists recruited to deal with the embodied trauma of BIPOC people are calling for a shift from trauma-centered care to healing-centered engagement.[9] They agree that there must be an opportunity to retrieve lost stories, to share details of those stories that explain what happened to people. These counter-narratives are difficult to sustain in a society that relies on its commonly held stock stories that uphold the status quo and white advantage.

Professor Lee Anne Bell and her creative team identified storytelling categories and developed a counter-storytelling process that empowers BIPOC people to confront racism with their own narratives.[10] The first story category is the stock story (i.e., the American Dream), "told by the dominant group, passed on through historical and literary documents, . . . public rituals, [and] law."[11] Stock stories have the power of social enforcement through public education, selective hagiography, and familiarity.

Concealed stories "coexist alongside the stock stories but most often remain in the shadows, hidden from mainstream view. . . . Though invisible to those in the mainstream, concealed stories are circulated, told and retold by people in the margins whose experiences and aspirations they express and honor."[12] In concealed stories, marginalized groups shed the mantle of inferiority and speak to the power of their culture and kin. Langston Hughes' poem "A Dream Deferred" is a direct counter-story to the American Dream mythologies.

---

8. Debra Hosseini, "Storytelling, Neuroscience, and Healing Trauma," *The Art of Autism*, October 1, 2013, https://the-art-of-autism.com/storytelling-neuroscience-and-healing-trauma/.

9. Rowe and Woodson.

10. Lee Ann Bell, *Storytelling for Social Justice: Connecting Narrative and the Arts in AntiRacist Teaching*, 2nd ed. (New York: Routledge, 2020).

11. Bell, 18.

12. Bell, 19.

The third category of storytelling that Bell identifies is the resistance story. These are stories of how marginalized groups resist their oppression. However, the tendency is to focus on individual heroes. Such focus diminishes the power of collective cultural resistance to oppression. One such example is the filmed story of Harriet Tubman. Everyone loves the story of one black woman freeing slaves all by herself, but they are less likely to know or support the story of Haiti's rebellion against slaveholding nations, including how Haiti ultimately won those battles as a community.

Finally, we recognize emerging/transforming stories that oppose and challenge stock stories, create new stories, and inspire imaginative constructions of a new society. The new stories imagine what it would be like if the empty promises ensconced in America's founding documents were fulfilled. I have always said that we can't inhabit what we have not imagined. Villages under siege know what they don't want. Through transforming stories, they draw blueprints of what they do want so that construction can begin. When we tell the stories of "what happened,"

> We . . . can recognize the divine within, as well as promote our community members' interdependence and interconnectedness—truly embodying the African proverb, "I am because we are and since we are, therefore I am."[13]

Stories are part of the cultural history of Africans in the Diaspora. In West African contexts, griots were the cultural, political, and historical keepers of the stories. They passed the information down through oral traditions with the intent of preserving village and cultural history. Griots wove stories of marriages, battles, and tribal lineage with skill and an eye toward entertainment. They had flexibility in the telling of the story, because the story was a living reenactment of life in community.

Unlike many of the stories with which we grew up, there was not a fixed moral lesson at the end. The stories were creatively open to trickster elements, surprise endings, and updates. What was important was that the community held the stories with intentions of healing the broken places

13. Rowe and Woodson.

in unique and unexpected ways. "Telling another human being what has taken place in one's life can be an important part of healing from trauma and can lay the foundation for new stories about what the future holds."[14]

There is a future because the stories are not locked up within our individual lives. Instead, they are held as precious elements of communal wisdom. Our stories do not need opportunities for neat resolution; they just need to be told over and over again. They need to be heard and pondered before the dancing begins—and the dancing will begin again because when we lose hope and joy as individuals, the community digs deep into its shared resources and starts the beat yet again. They tap their feet and drum the promises of God.

The reality is that the life journey is a mix of joy, trouble, loss, gain, growth, and diminishment. Recovery from trauma begins with understanding that trauma is part of a season of life, but it is not ultimate. It is not the final word. If we can leave behind imaginary constructs, like "whiteness" and "blackness" and "illegals," if we can reclaim and honor elders through our stories, if we can initiate rising generations into the ways of the elders, healing might just be possible.

Revival of Our Culture and Our Rituals

According to the healers we interviewed, culture is the primary vehicle for delivering healing. The overarching principle articulated here, that "culture is medicine," means that connecting with one's culture has both protective and therapeutic value, promoting both resilience to and recovery from traumatic events. The details of treatment will differ depending on the cultural specifics related to one's culture; however, the principle of culture as medicine is the same across Native cultures, according to the healers we interviewed. Thus, indigenous means of treatment through culture may include any or all of the following: language, traditional foods, ceremonies,

---

14. Andrea Blanch, Beth Filson, and Darby Penney, *Engaging Women in Trauma-Informed Peer Support: A Guidebook* (National Center for Trauma-Informed Care, 2012), 70, https://www.nasmhpd.org/sites/default/files/PeerEngagementGuide_Color_REVISED_10_2012.pdf.

traditional values, spiritual beliefs, history, stories, songs, traditional plants, and canoe journeys. Connecting Native patients with their Native culture promotes better health outcomes.[15]

CONNECTIONS HEAL BECAUSE trauma disconnects us from the vital force that flows through gathered minds, bodies, and hearts. When health systems don't include cultural realities as an integral aspect of healing, they miss the opportunity to utilize powerful disease-disrupting practices.

When I moved to Miami to practice law, I also started a homeless ministry with several friends. We would intercede on the beaches, where homeless hospital patients would be dumped at night. This was during the 1990s, and I assume that those practices have ended. But, at that point, if someone had no insurance, or the hospital needed the bed, impoverished people were unceremoniously left on beaches, some in wheelchairs, some bandaged and bleeding. My ministry partners and I gave them shelter in our own homes for the night and connected them to social services in the morning.

It occurred to my partners and me that we could probably be of more help if we could serve as volunteers in the chaplains' offices of local hospitals. I went to one hospital to talk with the supervising chaplain. I asked what I had to do to be allowed to serve as a volunteer. He barely looked up at me, saying, "Get your chicken and head up to the rooms. Nobody else asks me anything. They just bring their rituals and get started."

I left his office and went upstairs to see for myself. Sure enough, there were Santerían priests, indigenous healers, and vodun practitioners from Haiti. Everywhere I looked, I saw healing rituals from different cultures, while Western medicine continued as if nothing unusual was going on. Patients probably benefitted from both. Although I did not understand what I was seeing at the time, I now know that traditional healing ceremonies offer a sacred path toward the healing of group trauma.

Dr. Maria Yellow Horse Brave Heart has been writing and researching for years about the path toward healing for Native people. Included in

---

15. Deborah Bassett, Ursula Tsosie, and Sweetwater Nannauck, "'Our Culture Is Medicine': Perspectives of Native Healers on Posttrauma Recovery among American Indian and Alaska Native Patients," *Permanente Journal* 16, no. 1 (Winter 2012): 19–27, doi: 10.7812/tpp/11-123.

her work are returns to sacred places, ceremonies to honor great leaders, the training of facilitators to help with grief processing, and identifying strengths and rituals from traditional cultures. In some African diasporan cultures, where erasure of origins was almost total, DNA tests would be part of the process of healing. Brave Heart's chart below could be used by any community working to heal from trauma.[16]

Brave Heart notes that ceremonies may help in the healing process by changing brain chemistry and calming traumatic brain responses. She also states that these healing rituals reduced the groups' sense of responsibility to undo a painful history; lessened shame, stigma, and anger; and increased joy.

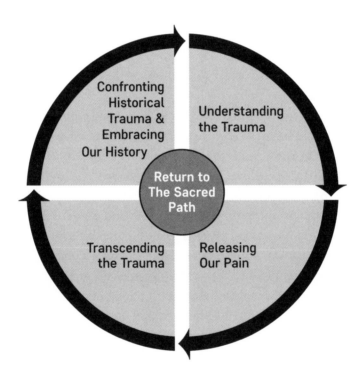

16. A version of this chart was published in Maria Yellow Horse Brave Heart, "The Return to the Sacred Path: Healing the Historical Trauma and Historical Unresolved Grief Response among the Lakota through a Psychoeducational Group Intervention," *Smith College Studies in Social Work* 68, no. 3, 287–305.

Performing Joy

Where society has told us to "be quiet," and that we're "too loud" and "too different," it is an act of resistance to revel in the joy that they have spent much of history trying to take away from us.[17]

"When we acknowledge that we exist in an anti-black world that is set up to ensure we do not live, to choose life and to choose to enjoy any aspect of that life is a radical act. . . . Amplifying black joy is not about dismissing or creating an 'alternative' black narrative that ignores the realities of our collective pain; rather, it is about holding the pain and injustices we experience as black folks around the world in tension with the joy we experience in pain's midst. It's about using that joy as an entry into understanding the oppressive forces we navigate through as a means to imagine and create a world free of them."[18]

PERFORMING JOY AS a path toward healing is discussed within the context of black community, but applies to all marginalized or traumatized people. Our current circumstances require resilience and the steadfast belief that joy is a healing inner event and a spiritual practice. I am using the black community to exemplify this performance of humanity despite unrelenting oppression, but other villages can substitute their own practices of joy.

BIPOC folks who remember the ways of the elders have seen it in action. Performance of joy while the wounds are still being inflicted is not a display of otherworldly strength. It is an act of faith that God will not give us more than we can bear. Expressions of joy by communities subjected to violence are often misinterpreted.

---

17. Chante Joseph, "What Black Joy Means—and Why It's More Important than Ever," *Vogue*, July 29, 2020, https://www.vogue.co.uk/arts-and-lifestyle/article/what-is-black-joy.

18. Kleaver Cruz, as quoted in Joseph. Kleaver Cruz is a New York writer who started the Black Joy Project, a digital and real-world movement to center black joy.

In a capitalistic society founded on competition, privatization and small family units, collective joy—as opposed to individual happiness—signals both personal resilience and political rebellion.[19]

Moreover, we know that although we have bodies, and a corporeal witness as human beings, we are also energy, consciousness, and spirit with connections to quantum possibilities. Although relief seems to be an impossibility, we know that we are embedded in a quantum world that is nothing but possibility. When we let the social disorder define us, we begin to vibrate at a lower frequency and become heavy of spirit. The more that we try to fit into the dream world of attachment and material things, the less joy we have.

The Civil Rights movement fought for justice and freedom, but when the leaders were assassinated, the goals were translated into material inclusion and entitlements (from voting and integration to eating in public restaurants). The Black Lives Matter movement tries to stop the killing of innocent black and brown bodies. Both movements have been necessary and empowering, but real joy and real freedom will come when we reclaim our continuum thinking and our ancestral connections to sacred realities.

Ossie Davis (1917–2005) said, "I find in being black a thing of beauty: a joy; a strength; a secret cup of gladness."[20] This secret cup of joy is not the momentary sip that happiness gives, but a source of refreshment from deep wells. Poet Jericho Brown describes the difference between joy and happiness:

> In the church where I was raised, adults made a sharp distinction between joy and happiness. Happiness felt good, but it was temporary, and because it was temporary, there was something about it not to be trusted. . . . Joy, as it was explained to me, is a spiritual thing.[21]

19. Janey Stephenson, "Why Joy Is the Perfect Resistance to a Politics of Fear," *Waging Nonviolence: People Powered News & Analysis*, August 9, 2017, https://waging-nonviolence.org/2017/08/joy-resistance-politics-fear-fascism/.

20. Ossie Davis, *Life Lit by Some Large Vision: Selected Speeches and Writings*, ed. Ruby Dee (New York: Atria, 2006), 253.

21. Jericho Brown, "The Long Distance Between Poems," *Boston Review*, April 29, 2016, http://bostonreview.net/poetry/NPM-2016-jericho-brown-long-distance-between-poems.

Personal and communal joy require authenticity. We have to stop performing the blackness that whiteness created, the stereotypes and secret-keeping.[22] We have to sing ourselves sane and dance ourselves free. Each act of public joy is one step closer to that risky leap toward transcendence.

As for the ways communities sustain themselves economically, we have to allow joy to generate jobs and alternative avenues of labor while we journey beyond the mandates of imperialism, capitalism, colonization, and competition. To return to Dedan's question to Belvie, "What does healing look like?"

Here are ways we can perform joy as a healing ritual:

1. We can reconnect to the earth, grow our own food, and recognize our embeddedness in the natural world.
2. We can recognize that the social inducement to accumulate anything other than wisdom is foolish. There is nothing that we brought to this world, and nothing that we take with us.
3. We can rely on the healing effects of joy as the blessed unfolding of unlimited possibilities and the reunion of the scattered.

Performing joy offers healing from our addictive engagement with domination systems. We are not required to fight for our reality; we can just live it. We can be weird and whole and as shapeshifting as necessary, for we are being called to another purpose. We are being invited to awaken to our true nature as spirit beings, energy sharers, and prophets of potential. The joy spoken of in Holy Scripture is accessible, but also has a certain "beyondness" to it: The world didn't give it and the world can't take it away. As we hear from Jesus in John 16:22: "So you have pain now; but I will see you again and your hearts will rejoice, and no one will take your joy from you."

Even the epigenetic changes that trauma can induce might contribute to our strength. Dr. Rachel Yehuda says,

> I think the purpose of epigenetic changes . . . is simply to increase the repertoire of possible responses. I don't think it's meant to damage

22. Victor Anderson, *Beyond Ontological Blackness: An Essay on African American Religious and Cultural Criticism* (New York: Bloomsbury Academic, 2016).

or not damage people; it just—it expands the range of biologic responses. And that can be a very positive thing, when that's needed. Who would you rather be in a war zone with—somebody that's had previous adversity, knows how to defend themselves, or somebody that has never had to fight for anything, but might be very advantaged in many other social and cultural ways?[23]

I am a firm believer that difficulties make us stronger and more resilient as time goes on.

Finally, there is joy in cathartic spiritual practices and in the reclamation of cultural traditions, but there is another expression of joy that invites us to "come away for awhile." Reagan Jackson writes,

> We are living in a toxic environment . . . so the idea of taking a few hours to gather together with other black people, not to discuss race, not to [fuss] about white people, but to simply disengage from society's problems and dance and laugh and remember our own humanity is truly powerful. The very best way white people can show their allyship is by not interrupting that time, by not centering their needs to feel included or their desires to "help."[24]

Performing black joy in public also requires spiritual grounding in our history and legacy. We are not performing to please dominant culture. We are opening ourselves to release the pain and reconnect to community. As we sit with what is and what never should have been, our feet remember the call of the drums and we allow the s(S)pirit within to soar.

I have not included specific healing practices at the end of this chapter because communal healing is a process, not a practice. Throughout the chapter, I hope that you will find opportunities for reflection and receptivity to processes that orient us toward healing.

---

23. Yehuda.

24. Reagan Jackson, "The Necessity of Black Joy," *The Seattle Globalist*, July 18, 2017, http://seattleglobalist.com/2017/07/18/necessity-black-joy/67335.

Afrofuturism is more than just breaking down racial constructs, it is really a way of triggering the imagination so that people can look at themselves and celebrate. . . . It is about reclaiming humanity outside of these racial norms.

—Ytasha Womack

CHAPTER SIX

FUTURISM AND COSMIC REBIRTH

There are black people in the future.
　　　　　　　　　—Alisha B. Wormsley

It is a radical act for black people to imagine having a future.
　　　　　　　　　—Nalo Hopkinson

WHEN CRISIS IS the context for the past and present, hopeful people manage the now and imagine a future. The black women writers quoted above reference a multi-dimensional future that is within our collective reach. Ytasha Womack wants BIPOC folks to imagine more than they have been taught. She wants to loosen the restrictions of racial categories to encourage the emergence of cosmic elements of humanity. Alisha Wormsley, an interdisciplinary artist, wants to be sure that BIPOC folks survive, and so named her project "There are Black people in the Future." This is a mantra of reassurance and a public commitment to continue to exist. Writer and professor Nalo Hopkinson also weaves her stories of a future that includes thriving communities of color and culture. These artists are not describing extraordinary heroism or epic struggles against "the powers that be." Instead, they are highlighting the galactic transformations necessary to imagine more than past and present oppressions.

When I first conceived this book, I thought that it would end with the chapter on healing. It didn't take long to realize that although our hope of healing has dominated our dreams and our social narratives throughout my lifetime, those dreams have roots in the politics and social concerns of this present era. We have to imagine more peace than we currently have, and more justice than the mere conversion of racist policies will allow. A transformative change is needed!

Universal Patterns of Change and Transformation

As I noted in Chapter 3, Fr. Richard Rohr has identified what he describes as the universal wisdom pattern of change and transformation: order, disorder, and reorder. I consider crisis contemplation to be an aspect of disorder that prepares communities for a leap toward the future. This is a leap toward our beginnings. We are not just organisms functioning on a biological level; our sphere of being also includes stardust and consciousness. We all have a spark of divinity within, a flicker of Holy Fire that can be diminished, but never extinguished.

If we are treated as prey, stolen from our native lands, and killed without restraint by those agencies charged with the responsibility of keeping "order," our sense of empowerment and agency may wane. During a crisis, survival becomes the focus. Prey run from predators, and so, without realizing it, as we spiritually and actively seek to escape the clutches of white supremacy, we begin to think of ourselves as hapless victims of a prowling beast that cannot be stopped. When parents of BIPOC children give "the talk" today, we are teaching our children to survive predation.[1] We have to imagine more!

As I have previously written, we have to imagine a new future before we can build and inhabit it, but how do we imagine what we have never

---

1. "The talk" is given by BIPOC parents to protect their children from police violence: "Keep your hands at ten and two and don't look at them. No smart talk. No fast moves. Don't open the glove compartment without asking." There are many variations of the talk.

known? Can we engage the imaginative constructs of Afrofuturism as a vehicle for creating a future?

Afrofuturism

> Afrofuturism—broadly speaking—takes black histories and realities and adds a dose of magic, mysticism, superpowers, or all three to create new worlds where the protagonists are black people. These stories can be sci-fi, they can be horror, they can imagine a past that never happened or a distant future that by today's standards seems impossible.[2]

ALTHOUGH THE WORD "Afrofuturism" was formally coined by Mark Dery in 1994,[3] as a genre, it existed well before it was formally named.

> [The genre stretches] back to the subversive, future forward aesthetic of artists like Sun Ra, Parliament Funkadelic and novelist Octavia E. Butler's 1970s "Patternist" series. For Afrodiasporic artists, the genre provides a fertile landscape to dream up a future outside of the limits of white supremacy; it is powerful because it dares to dream a future for Afrodiasporic people at all.[4]

Afrofuturism describes "speculative fiction that treats African-American themes and addresses African-American concerns within the context of twentieth-century techno-culture."[5] Today, the genre is even

---

2. Elizabeth Wellington and Raishad Hardnett, "Afrofuturism Is All around Us and We Don't Even Know It," *The Philadelphia Inquirer*, February 26, 2020, https://www.inquirer.com/columnists/afrofuturism-future-the-black-tribbles-black-panther-octavia-butler-20200226.html.

3. Mark Dery, "Black to the Future: Interviews with Samuel R. Delany, Greg Tate, and Tricia Rose" in *Flame Wars: The Discourse of Cyberculture* (Durham, NC: Duke University Press, 1994), 179–222.

4. Arielle Gray, "These 2 Poets Imagine Our Afrofuturist Possibilities Past Trauma in 'Spirit,'" *NPR/WBUR*, October 10, 2019, https://www.wbur.org/artery/2019/10/10/spirit-preview-isgm.

5. Felicia L. Harris, "'Tell Me the Story of Home': Afrofuturism, Eric Killmonger, and Black American Malaise," *Review of Communication* 20, no. 3 (July 20, 2020): 278–285, https://doi.org/10.1080/15358593.2020.1778069.

more comprehensive, and yet we continue to host Dery's foundational question: "Can a community whose past has been deliberately rubbed out, and whose energies have subsequently been consumed by the search for legible traces of its history, imagine possible futures?"[6] The answer is a resounding "yes." But first, we must begin to see ourselves differently: not as prey, not in a constant state of resistance, but as time travelers and dreamers, conjurers and pilgrims.

Seeing Ourselves Differently

We have an urgent need to identify as the cosmic beings we actually are with a huge role in the cosmos.[7]

FUTURIST ARTIST AND photographer Mikael Owunna offers us the opportunity to see ourselves whole and cosmically connected through his luminescent photography. He calls himself an Astro-Black mythologist, a term coined by scholar Marques Redd. According to Owunna,

The *astro* communicates how human life in many African traditions is in constant communication with interstellar and planetary contexts, the *Black* evokes Blackness as a divine, cosmic principle of the universe, and African *mythology* serves as a mode of knowledge that fuses science, religion, and art to transform human consciousness.[8]

Owunna helps us to envision this transformation through stunning visual depictions of dark bodies illuminated as astral projections of a sacred cosmos. Through his lens, dark bodies become not just dreamers

---

6. Harris.

7. Nancy Ellen Abrams, as quoted in Cathy Lynn Grossman, "What's Your 'Cosmic Identity'? Philosopher Says You Have One," *The Washington Post*, April 24, 2015, https://www.washingtonpost.com/national/religion/whats-your-cosmic-identity-philosopher-says-you-have-one/2015/04/24/f34d05fc-eaaf-11e4-8581-633c536add4b_story.html.

8. Jon Feinstein, "Astro-Black Mythology: In Conversation with Mikael Owunna," *Humble Arts Foundation*, September 24, 2020, http://hafny.org/blog/2020/9/astro-black-mythology-in-conversation-with-mikael-owunna.

about the future, but performers and conjuring progenitors of our cosmic potential. He says,

> My work seeks to elucidate an emancipatory vision of possibility that pushes Black people beyond all boundaries, restrictions, and frontiers. In this vision, we open our eyes to the cosmic forms inherent in our Blackness. By opening our eyes, we illuminate the universe and reveal the existence of all things in their formation.[9]

The exciting thing about these photographic astral images is that we cannot see this work without expanding our cosmic sense of black/brown humanity. These images are not an attempt to bravely convince others that dark bodies deserve respect in the public square. Instead, Owunna offers a vision of sacred self to those who have been systematically hunted and destroyed. Owunna says, "The question I asked myself here was: how can I transfigure Black bodies from sites of death and state violence into transcendent forms, into vessels of eternal, cosmic life?"[10]

Owunna's photography gives us a glimpse of embodied mystery. Other artists also give us a glimpse of our cosmic connections. Cliff Berrien, artist and musician, uses digital cosmic projections to unveil our relatedness to the universe.[11] Both offer a completely different manifestation of being "woke." When I look at Owunna's or Berrien's work, I see the illumination of cosmic potential in dark bodies. This light reveals who we have been and what could be possible when we consider our cosmic origins.

The Blessing of Liminality

LIMINALITY IS AN attribute of ambiguity that occurs in a rite of passage, when participants have left behind their pre-ritual status but have not yet transitioned to their post-ritual status.

---

9. Feinstein.
10. Feinstein.
11. For a sample of his collaborative work, see the cover of my book *Race and the Cosmos* (Albuquerque, NM: CAC Publishing, 2020).

Liminal entities are neither here nor there; they are betwixt and between the positions assigned and arrayed by law, custom, convention, and ceremonial. . . . Thus, liminality is frequently likened to death, to being in the womb, to invisibility, to darkness, to bisexuality, to the wilderness, and to an eclipse of the sun or moon.[12]

When a village experiences a crisis that shatters normalcy, it finds itself in liminal spaces. The crisis shatters suppositions, identities, and reality structures. Often, the community experiences the end of one reality and entry into a state of being that Victor Turner (1920–1983) defined as betwixt and between states of reality. As a group, we are neither here nor there. According to Turner,

Liminars are stripped of status and authority, removed from a social structure maintained and sanctioned by power and force, and leveled to a homogeneous social state through discipline and ordeal.[13]

As community members, we are in the midst of a ritual passage from one state of being to another. Whether the passage is from wise elder in a West African village to slavery on a Maryland plantation, or keeper of the sacred land in the Cherokee Nation to death march survivor on the Trail of Tears, contemplation in liminal spaces seems like a rebirthing process.

A liminal space is the time between the "what was" and the "next." It is a place of transition, a season of waiting, and not knowing. Liminal space is where all transformation takes place, if we learn to wait and let it form us.[14]

During the transition, the breaking that we experience is formative and healing. After all, what is liminality but a transition between one state

---

12. Victor Turner, *The Ritual Process: Structure and Anti-Structure* (Chicago: University of Chicago Press, 1969), 95.

13. Victor Turner, *Process, Performance, and Pilgrimage: A Study in Comparative Symbology* (New Delhi: Concept, 1979), 149.

14. Jon DeWaal and Shonnie Scott, "What Is a Liminal Space?" *Liminal Space*, https://inaliminalspace.org/about-us/what-is-a-liminal-space/.

of reality and another, betwixt and between the splitting of the cocoon and the release of the butterfly? When we emerge, it is hoped that we will have shed our gnarly caterpillar ways for wings so that we can fly. Change from one state of being to another always requires some type of transformation.

Although we pretend that our current reality is the only one that exists, science tells us that there are multiple dimensions and a fluidity to the life space that allows us to rise above our circumstances when the time is right. Africans in the Diaspora took those stories seriously. The stories of flying Africans are a part of the oral history of enslaved people in the Americas. As a child, I read stories about flying Africans and would ask my grandmother, "Did they really fly?" She would respond: "It was flying time and so they flew." In other words, you do what you have to do, but not until it is time.

According to the stories, enslaved men and women flew back to Africa. In my creative imagination, I like to think that they did not fly back to the familiar. Instead, I picture them soaring beyond the chains and beatings to the realm of the ancestors for consultations on the plight and future of the community. I imagine flight past this global society, toward a society fueled by creativity instead of production. These communities would be formed by like-minded spirits, not same-colored bodies.

Layli Maparyan states, "Humanity is in the process of evolving toward global society and planetary identity based on global, even cosmic citizenship."[15] We are in the midst of a cosmic shift. An old order is fading away and a new one is not yet on the horizon. We have grown weary of our quarantines, our Zoom contacts, and our restrictions, so we rebel, wanting a quick fix, a temporary solution. What is called for in times like these is a deep dive into unknowing, a trusting, and a liminal float in spiritual depths that sustain our collective wellbeing.

Sacred Journey

We have not been invited to build permanent habitations on this journey. Our engagement with the powers is intense and transitory.

---

15. Layli Maparyan, *The Womanist Idea* (New York: Routledge, 2012), 4.

Sometimes the questions we are being asked to resolve in public life have jokes for answers or no answer at all.[16]

As a community, we have embarked on a sacred journey. Accordingly, we cannot stay in comfort or familiarity. The human family is headed toward a higher state of belonging and reunion. Afrofuturism helps us to imagine this journey. Writer Mohale Mashigo argues that Africans still living on the continent don't need Afrofuturism as their primary lens. Instead, post-colonial Africa needs a better present:

> Afrofuturism is an escape for those who find themselves in the minority and divorced or violently removed from their African roots, so they imagine a "black future" where they aren't a minority and are able to marry their culture with technology. That is a very important story and it means a lot to many people.[17]

Mashigo is describing an African diasporic need to fill in the gaps of culture, history, and lineage, while she suggests that Africans living on the continent need a present-day reclamation of land and communal formation that honors tribal realities, as well as broader economic and spiritual alliances and the centering of African culture.

I agree that we all need a better "now," but it does not have to come at the expense of a richly envisioned future. I also recognize the experiential differences that Mashigo suggests, but contend that the common themes among African people are displacement and crisis, not geographic location. Africans, whether on the continent or off, are dealing with historical, communal, and traumatic crises that alter our sense of self and our ability to imagine a future.

---

16. Barbara A. Holmes, "Still on the Journey: Moral Witness, Imagination, and Improvisation in Public Life," in Marcia Y. Riggs and James Samuel Logan, eds., *Ethics that Matters: African, Caribbean, and African American Sources* (Minneapolis: Fortress, 2012), 238.

17. Mohale Hashigo, "Afrofuturism Is Not for Africans Living in Africa," *Intruders* (Johannesburg: Picador Africa, 2018), as excerpted in *The Johannesburg Review of Books*, October 1, 2018, https://johannesburgreviewofbooks.com/2018/10/01/afrofuturism-is-not-for-africans-living-in-africa-an-essay-by-mohale-mashigo-excerpted-from-her-new-collection-of-short-stories-intruders/.

Afrofuturism offers mythologies, shamanic journeys, and the creative arts to prepare us for the transcendent leap. Through imagination and the telling of our stories, we can honor our specific needs while affirming our shared need for a cosmic rebirth. Ytasha Womack gives us a glimpse of what a cosmic rebirthing would include: a valuing of the Divine Feminine, engagements with the mystical as an everyday practice, and a deflation of the power of "race" in our lives.

Womack emphasizes the fact that "race," or the categorization of human beings by the color of their skin, is a flawed technology invented to justify the slave trade and other oppressions.[18] We have the opportunity to center our cosmic potential instead.

Honoring the Luminous Womanist

THE SURVIVAL OF African people in the Diaspora is not a result of heroic resilience or serendipity. It is grounded in the spiritual intention of communities of color and culture, who would not allow their sons and daughters to become fodder for colonizers. When the men of a community are the focus of state violence, when they are being killed with impunity, studded and castrated, broken and hung, that's when the wonder of womanism arises.

By "wonder," I mean the ability to embody the sacred and to ignite faith in the unseen. Through ingenuity and manipulation of systems set up to destroy, black women protected their communities. They accomplished these feats for and with the entire community, while honoring their men. They still sustain, console, foretell, and revive villages on the brink of emotional and spiritual despair. It is a wonder that the woman who washes your clothes and tends your children is connected directly to the cosmic and the ancestral. If you look closely, you can see the light shining round about her and the other members of her community: light as energy, light as life, light as a stimulus for the creative genesis of darkness.

We are used to discussions of the Divine Feminine as a white feminist vision of power and sacredness that often overshadows the practical

18. Ytasha L. Womack, "Insights into Afrofuturism," *Adler Planetarium*, February 10, 2019, https://www.adlerplanetarium.org/blog/insights-into-afrofuturism/.

and everyday mysticism of BIPOC women. Although images of the Black Madonna can be found throughout Europe, she is seldom the focus of the Western cultural imagination. Ultimately, we find our own pathways toward wholeness based on our experiences, not our skin color. Accordingly, some BIPOC women identify as feminists, others choose womanism, even others resist all efforts to fit their humanity into neat categories.

I choose womanism as my means of interpreting the Divine Feminine in dark bodies because it encodes the mysteries of life as well as a focus on community rather than individual rights. I am also less than confident that I would find safety and common purpose in feminism with white women whose husbands, fathers, and sons monopolize the patriarchy and continue to perpetuate violence against BIPOC communities.

When I use the term "womanist," I am referencing Black women who prioritize community values and who are willing to embrace their darkness and let their little light shine, even in the midst of systemic attempts to extinguish the very essence of their being. Alice Walker's definition of womanism only codified wisdom passed down through the generations. As helpful as it was for Walker to define the attributes of womanism in a literary way, we all knew what our elders taught: We walk by faith, rule by light, and embrace the mysteries of darknesses that are cosmic and pervasive.

Layli Maparyan describes the wonder of womanists who recognize Innate Divinity and Inner Light as a spiritual practice available to anyone who chooses to recognize "the inherently luminous nature of humans and all creation."[19] Maparyan also describes the emergence of an egalitarian society as a luminous revolution, a movement away from materialism toward "luxocracy," a nonviolent social order grounded in spirituality and the "rule by light."[20] So there we have it: We can embrace the healing elements of darkness, shadow, and eclipse, while leading by light.

---

19. Maparyan, 14.
20. Maparyan, 3.

Cosmic Rebirth through Mysticism

For what is the mystical life but God coming to do what we cannot do?

—Ruth Burrows, OCD

All people must learn to draw upon their own Implanted Spirit, which is the only thing that will help them in the long run anyway. Jesus gives them the courage to trust their own "inner Christ"—and not just its outer manifestation in himself.[21]

COSMIC REBIRTHING REQUIRES a reclamation of everyday mysticism. I am an everyday mystic, perhaps not of the ilk that Karl Rahner described, but a mystic nonetheless. I was born into a family of shamans, root workers, and healers. These women and men saw beyond the veil and mediated the realms of life after life. They knew how to cure you of what ailed you, spiritually and in the natural world. The mystics that I knew could get a prayer through, birth a baby, and bring you a message or warning from the other side. They were amazing and sometimes a little bit scary.

Although I love the signs and wonders of the Pentecostal and Charismatic movements, their dramatic conversions, prophecy, and intoxication in the Spirit, I am more familiar with ordinary life spaces that are permeated with mystery. I am describing mysticism as a natural part of my everyday life—no weird music, no sweeping cloaks, no spooky incantations, just a recognition of the Implanted Spirit that Rohr references. As John Crockett notes, "'Mystical' means 'with closed lips.' . . . mysticism is the thought-stopping realization that reality cannot be captured with words or concepts."[22]

If we are to remember our cosmic origins, if we are to recognize the star-stuff in our bodies, if we are to understand our biogenetic connections one to another, then we need more mystery, not less. During a crisis, we survive in community through the contemplative enhancement of

---

21. Richard Rohr, *The Universal Christ: How a Forgotten Reality Can Change Everything We See, Hope For, and Believe* (New York: Convergent, 2018), 76.
22. Crockett.

discernment, by tapping into spiritual wisdom sources, by re-ordering our taken-for-granted values, and by reliance upon the Spirit within.

Mysticism reminds us that the boundaries between this life and the life beyond are permeable, and that our power is not seeded in what is bestowed by politicians and society, but to everyone willing and ready to recognize the moves of an active Holy Spirit. Mysticism helps people under siege to transcend hatred and sustain hope, to meet devastating violence with communal resilience and peaceful resistance.

By being receptive to the things that we don't understand, we fling open the center of our being to the mysteries of the Divine. I will tell you a story of an actual event that I cannot explain. It was the Feast of the Immaculate Conception of the Blessed Virgin Mary, in December. At the time, I was teaching at Memphis Theological Seminary.

I admit that, during this period of time, I had tucked the mystical away. I didn't think that I had any need for it as I juggled the responsibilities of being a new professor, teaching academic subjects while trying to engage students and grade their work. I was about to go to lunch when a friend came by and invited me to go with her to a noontime Mass at St. Mary's in downtown Memphis.

The priest who was officiating had been assigned to Africa for years and was called back to the States for a brief time before he returned to the continent. He was offering communion. He lifted a wafer of rather large circumference, and, as he lifted it, his feet slowly rose above the floor. The sight was stunning. His eyes were uplifted, his feet defying gravity, wafer held high. I didn't dare turn away.

I used my stage-whisper voice, without shifting my gaze, and asked my friend, "Do you see this!?"

"Yes," she replied.

Slowly, he descended, and it seemed as if time stood still. Finally, we broke our stare to look around the room. Had anyone else seen this?! No one seemed to have noticed anything unusual. When we got outside, tears were running down our faces. We hugged one another, went back to work, and did not speak of the occurrence again. But why did we see it?

There is no good ending to a story that includes an inbreaking mystery with no rational explanation, and so I offer this litany.

A Litany

One: We are unique, and ordinary, mystics in the making, flowing from one state of existence to another, inhabiting the ordinary, touching the eternal.

Many: We are embedded in a continuum of life, related to the Divine, the earth, and our neighbors.

One: We did not just burst out of nowhere. We will not disappear when we die.

Many: We come from particularity and community, mystery and cosmic realities. We have a future! Thanks be!

Decentering Race: Welcoming Cosmic Rebirth

> Racism for Whites has been like a crazy uncle who has been locked away for generations in the hidden attic of our collective social reality. This old relative has been a part of the family for a long time. Everyone knows he's living with us, because we bring him food and water occasionally, but nobody wants to take him out in public. He is an embarrassment and a pain to deal with, yet our little family secret is that he is rich and the rest of us are living, either consciously or unconsciously, off the wealth and power he accumulated in his heyday. Even though many of us may disapprove of the tactics he used to gain his fortune, few of us want to be written out of his will. The legacy of racism, which has been fueled and legitimized by our assumption of rightness, has haunted the house of collective White identity for centuries.[23]

As HOWARD NOTES, the "house of collective White identity" is haunted by the myths that surround the idea of "race." However, there are benefits coming if the heirs of white oppression can stop pretending that there is no such uncle in the attic. The legacy of race and racism also continues to

---

23. Gary R. Howard, *We Can't Teach What We Don't Know: White Teachers, Multiracial Schools* (New York: Teachers College Press, 1999), 59.

haunt brown and black communities, even as they find their voices, their second wind, and power in the diversity of their multiple identities.

The rising generations are insisting, as a public mantra and mandate, that their black and brown lives matter. Moreover, they are unwilling to relentlessly battle the shape-shifting ghosts of race-based tyranny. Instead, these freedom seekers are holding up a blood-stained banner that centers their humanity and cosmic connections, while they declare their commitment to the well-being of the planet and all its inhabitants.

This freedom is not just from racially based structural oppression, but also from the well-worn survival tactics of civil rights activists. Grateful for the sacrifices made to secure various rights, another generation focuses its attention on the wonder of a spiritually enlivened reality. Still others are seeking freedom from an "ole time religion" that is more culturally and politically committed to the status quo than to ecologies of care and compassion.

> When we allow other beings to exist on their own terms, when we listen to them without imposing our worldview onto them, when we free them from our demands, we also free ourselves to participate fully, with them, in life's improvisational creativity.[24]

This creativity is an expression of the art of being, a reflection of joint purposes and communal manifestations of rebirthing. And so we wait and contemplate while cycles of crisis and wellbeing, stagnation and revival help us to leap from what was to what can be.

Summary

THE BIG QUESTIONS taunt us. How do we heal from social disorder? How do we trust one another again? How do we unveil a transformed and transforming future? The truth of the matter is that if I am going to survive, I had better have a spiritual regimen that strengthens my immune

---

24. Crockett.

system, fortifies my resolve, beckons the ancestors, and connects me to the creative spirit of all life—and if I don't do that now, later will be too late.

I bring to this discussion my white supremacy-oriented education and terminal degree in theology. I also bring my mothers and other mothers, shamans and root women. I know who I am, but can seldom inhabit that space fully and peacefully. Like a film projected on a movie screen, so much has been projected on the screen of my life that I sometimes don't know who I am, or which me to bring forward, but I do know what I need and what is missing.

As people of color/culture, we need several things that are not readily available. We need an understanding of our ritual history and spiritual practices. We need a way to situate ourselves as fully human and cosmic beings. We need to know how to heal our wounds and bring solace to our community. Also, we need to consider whether or not some of us can temporarily pause energy-sapping activist practices so that we can breathe and be. Every once in a while, I need to crawl into the cosmic outline of human possibility and make a home there until the morning comes.

And if, after several decades, we still find ourselves in places of death and destruction despite all the singing and marching; if, in fact, we find our mother Rizpah fighting on a hill to protect what is left of our bones; then, with all the might that we can muster, we will have to make the transcendent leap toward an unseen future. We leap, trusting the glory of ancestral guidance, the blessed hope of the dawning of a new world order, and the promises of God.

—— *Afrofuturism and Cosmic Rebirth* ——

Practices

1. I have discussed cosmic rebirth as an aspect of Afrofuturism and the reclamation of an African past and future. What does your futurism look like?

    a. From your cultural perspective, who are your superheroes and why?

    b.   What is your community like in the future? What are you hoping
         for? Can you imagine and describe the church of the future?

2.   How do we craft the future that we want?

A Prayer of Gratitude

For the crises, the disruption of order,
and the plunge into contemplation,
we are grateful.
For the welcoming darkness
and the wounds that bring us
to a place of unknowing,
we thank God!
For the nurture of our many villages
of belonging, we are grateful.
For healing that comes in unexpected ways,
and the imaginative pathways
of futurism and cosmic rebirth,
thanks be.

ABOUT THE AUTHOR

Rev. Dr. Barbara A. Holmes is a spiritual teacher and writer who focuses on African American spirituality, mysticism, cosmology, and culture. A faculty member of the Center for Action and Contemplation's Living School, she is President Emerita of United Theological Seminary of the Twin Cities and served as Vice President of Academic Affairs and Dean of Memphis Theological Seminary. Dr. Holmes was called to ministry while working as a lawyer who specialized in civil litigation, corporate, and appellate practice. She was ordained in the Latter Rain Apostolic Holiness Church in Dallas, Texas and also has the privilege of call in the United Church of Christ and the Disciples of Christ. Dr. Holmes has worked with homeless missions, HIV/AIDS support groups, and international ministries in Kenya and Japan. The author of five books and numerous articles, her publications include *Liberation and the Cosmos: Conversations with the Elders, Joy Unspeakable: Contemplative Practices of the Black Church,* and *Race and the Cosmos: An Invitation to View the World Differently.* Learn more about Dr. Holmes at drbarbaraholmes.com.